PENGUIN BOOKS

HOW TO WATCH TV NEWS

Neil Postman is chairman of the Department of Communication Arts at New York University and founder of its program in Media Ecology. He is the author of nineteen books, including *Amusing Ourselves to Death* and *Technopoly*. In 1986, he won the George Orwell Award for Clarity in Language.

Steve Powers is an award-winning journalist with more than thirty years' experience in radio and television news, including as a correspondent for Fox Television News and the ABC Information Radio Network, and host of a top-rated morning talk show. Powers earned his Ph.D. in media studies from New York University in 1987.

HOW TO WATCH

TV NEWS

Neil Postman and *Steve Powers*

PENGUIN BOOKS

PENGUIN BOOKS
Published by the Penguin Group
Penguin Books USA Inc.,
375 Hudson Street, New York, New York 10014, U.S.A.
Penguin Books Ltd, 27 Wrights Lane, London W8 5TZ, England
Penguin Books Australia Ltd, Ringwood, Victoria, Australia
Penguin Books Canada Ltd, 10 Alcorn Avenue,
Toronto, Ontario, Canada M4V 3B2
Penguin Books (N.Z.) Ltd, 182–190 Wairau Road,
Auckland 10, New Zealand

Penguin Books Ltd, Registered Offices:
Harmondsworth, Middlesex, England

First published in Penguin Books 1992

5 7 9 10 8 6 4

LIBRARY OF CONGRESS CATALOGING IN PUBLICATION DATA
Postman, Neil.
How to watch TV news / Neil Postman and Steve Powers.
p. cm.
Includes index.
ISBN 0 14 01.3231 7
1. Television broadcasting of news—United States—Social aspects.
2. Television broadcasting of news—United States—Psychological
aspects. 3. Content analysis (Communication). I. Powers, Steve,
Ph.D. II. Title.
PN4888.T4P58 1992
070.1'95—dc20   92-6915

Printed in the United States of America
Set in Bauer Bodoni
Designed by Claire Naylon Vaccaro

ACKNOWLEDGMENTS

We wish to acknowledge the assistance of six people who generously provided us with their time and expertise: Professor Jay Rosen of New York University, especially for his help on Chapter 8; Professor Paul Thaler of Mercy College for his research on television in the courtroom and even for allowing us to use a few of his own words; Dr. Eva Berger of Tel Aviv University for providing a continuous flow of constructive criticism; Sheri Powers, whose insights helped guide us; Dr. Harry Royson for his inspiration; and Janet Sternberg of New York University for her editorial skills, and especially for her speedy and creative use of a word processor.

CONTENTS

CONTENTS

viii

PREFACE

This book was written by two men who have different kinds of knowledge about television but whose point of view is similar. Without the similarity we would not be of interest to each other. Without the differences we probably would not be of interest to the reader. One of us—Neil Postman—is an academic who has written books on the effects of media and, especially, on how television has altered various forms of social life. Although he once had a television show of his own (forty-eight half-hour programs under the aegis of "Sunrise Semester"), he is not skilled in the art of using television as a medium of communication. The other—Steve Powers—is a television journalist. He has a Ph.D. in media studies but has spent most of his professional life as a practitioner of both radio and television journalism. Postman's head is filled with theories, historical knowledge, and visions of what an awesome technology like television ought to do for a culture. Powers's head is filled with practical knowledge of what television, in fact, does, how it does it, and what it can do. We came to the conclusion some years ago that what television news says it is presenting and what it actually delivers are two different things. We concluded that a tidy and truthful book on how people should prepare themselves to interpret a television news show might be useful. The book at hand is the result.

Before saying anything else on the matter, we need to remark here that anyone who is not an avid reader of newspapers, magazines, and books is by definition unprepared to watch a television news show, and will always be. This point has been made many times with special force by such television journalists as Walter Cronkite, Bill Moyers, and Robert MacNeil. Anyone who relies exclusively on television for his or her knowledge of the world is making a serious mistake. Just as television can show things about the world that are not possible to experience through print, print can reveal complexities and facts that are not possible to show on television. Therefore, those who have not read about the world are limited in their capacity to understand what is seen on television. As an example, consider television's presentation of the uprising by Chinese students in Tiananmen Square. Anyone who watched diligently will never forget the image of a solitary student standing in front of a tank, obstructing it from proceeding. Mao Tse-tung preached that power begins behind the barrel of a gun. But this image, as media critic Jay Rosen once remarked, seemed to suggest that power also comes to those who *face* the barrel of a gun, provided that a camera catches them in the act, and that the image is witnessed by a vast audience. It was television journalism at its best. But if that is all someone knew about the student uprising, it wouldn't be very much. One would have to know something about who rules in China, and where these rulers came from, and by what authority or ideology they claim to rule, and how the students interpreted the meaning of freedom and democracy. These are complex matters that are beyond the scope of simple television newscasts, and must be learned through extensive reading of newspapers and books.

And so, the first lesson we have to teach is that preparation for watching a television news show begins with the preparation of one's mind through extensive reading. This lesson is of sufficient importance that we have seen fit to include it in our introduction. Having made this essential point, we will now turn our attention to all the others.

HOW TO WATCH

TV
NEWS

1

ARE YOU WATCHING TELEVISION OR IS TELEVISION WATCHING YOU?

Chances are you have at least one television set in your home that is used by most members of your family. Surveys of viewing patterns show that in an average household the television set is in use over seven hours a day. Nowadays, with the availability of cable, there are more programs than we have time to watch, even with the help of our VCRs. There are networks that carry only comedy, or news, or music, or courtroom proceedings, or financial information, or weather. There are even channels for shopping addicts who can't get enough buying done at their favorite stores. Insomniacs know "when sleep is stopping . . . you can always go shopping." The 92.1

million households in the United States with television sets have access to a constant stream of tempting programs that divert us every waking hour of our days. And of course there is the tremendous number of movies and other shows that can be rented on videotape or traded among aficionados. All of these programs are vying for your attention and time. Each show, series, and network is waving its electronic billboards at you, trying to grab your attention, in effect, saying, "Watch me, watch me." But your time is limited and valuable so you choose the programs you want to watch and, if you have a VCR, you can even choose when you want to watch them.

With such an awesome technology at our beck and call we tend to view television like any other appliance. Put it on when you want to, turn it off when you're through. Since you control it, you think that television is a one-way street . . . that you are using it . . . and it is not using you. But that is simply not the case. Your television set may not be able to see you eating snacks in your living room but it is still keeping an eye on you in different ways. The fact of the matter is that television not only delivers programs to your home but, more important to the advertising community, it also delivers you to a sponsor.

Advertisers and suppliers of programs spend a fortune slicing, dicing, chopping, and crunching numbers that will tell them what you are watching along with every bit of information about you they can get. They are not playing "Information Please." The kind of knowledge the advertisers seek gives them power and the more they know about you, the easier it is to sell you something. Developers of interactive television boast that in the future they will be able to send specific commercials to their subscribers based on the household's demographic composition. Theoretically, commercials for sneakers can be programmed to families with children who play basketball, while another commercial, perhaps for prescription drugs, can be sent to another family, composed of older people. That's in the future: in effect, custom-tailored sales pitches.

But right now advertisers have to rely on attracting a large-enough audience to their programs to deliver their messages. In fact, the reason popular TV series get on the air and stay there is that they can deliver the right audience for a sponsor, an audience that sees commercials and buys products or ideas. There is no escaping that fact: the whole point of television in America is to get you to watch so that programmers, performers, and others can rake in the money. Published reports say Merv Griffin, who originated the program "Wheel of Fortune," sold his company to Coca-Cola for $250 million, which, in turn, sold it to the Sony Corporation for even more. It has been reported in *Fortune* magazine that Oprah Winfrey has an estimated annual income of $40 million. Bill Cosby owns a healthy percentage of his television show and is a multimillionaire, sharing in the profits of his program, reruns, and syndication. All of which is to say that American television producers have been enormously successful in attracting large audiences. Their programs have been so popular that they threaten to undermine the TV systems of other countries throughout the world. For example, several European countries are trying to limit the number of American TV programs on the air so that more time can be given to their own programs, emphasizing their own cultural values. This is not easy to do since American programs, when in direct competition with "local" shows, consistently draw audiences away from home-grown products and create a demand for more American programs.

It might look like American TV producers are having everything their own way. Not so. The cost of producing sitcoms and other forms of popular entertainment has been growing. It now costs approximately $900,000 to produce a one-hour entertainment program. Producers claim they have to sell their programs to the networks, then syndicate them to make a profit. And while costs have been increasing, the audience for individual shows has declined as viewers find more and different channels and tapes to watch. It's no secret that news programs cost a lot less to produce than slick Hollywood dramas and laugh-tracked comedies. An hour of a news program, such as the CBS show "48 Hours," costs $500,000 or less. Compare that to an hour of so-called entertainment programming, with fancy production values, at about twice the cost, and you will know why the networks and other producers have found a new interest in news programs.

With the cost of news relatively inexpensive, there is more news being presented on television now than ever before. Not too long ago television news programs were money-losing products limited to a half-hour each day and the Sunday morning "public affairs" ghetto. But that has all changed. News programs are profit centers for the networks. There are all-news cable channels, special television news programs for children beamed into classrooms, and a plethora of network and syndicated news shows. Playing the numbers, there are "48 Hours," "60 Minutes," and "20/20." There are early-morning and late-night news programs. There are tabloid news shows, and programs featuring re-creations. Networks are making heavy profits from news, and on-air talent is being paid more than ever to communicate to the public. New technology has speeded the transmission of news into your home faster than ever before. Every night an estimated forty million people watch the news on the major networks and millions more watch local news coverage.

Moreover, the news audience is a highly desirable one. People who watch news tend to be more attentive to what is on the screen. They tend to be better educated and have more money to spend than the audiences for other shows. They are, therefore, a prime target for advertisers trying to reach an affluent market. Trying to reach the audience, sponsors are willing to pour money into well-produced commercials. These spots are often longer in length than most news stories and certainly cost more to produce than what's going into the content of the news. The commercials are fast-paced, exciting, and colorful, and, as a result, influence the way the news stories around them are produced. Propelled by the energy of the "Madison Avenue Shuffle," the whole news program takes on a rhythm and pace designed to hold interest and build viewership. More viewers, higher ratings, more advertising dollars, more profit, more similar programs to try to attract more viewers . . . ad infinitum.

So while there is a public service element deciding which news programs get on the air, the main factor is the profit motive. In fact, where news operations used to be considered a public service nonprofit operation of a station or network, in the new economics, news departments and programs are now expected to make money and they do. It's estimated that the ABC network made forty to fifty million dollars on commercials aired on the news alone last year. Executives at ABC have been quoted as saying that while being number one in the ratings used to be worth an additional $30 million for a network, it is no longer true. The new real standard of success, ABC says, is the demographic breakdown of the audience into age groups, with younger viewers favored by advertisers.

Of course, some news professionals believe that news departments dedicated to good solid journalism will bring credibility to the whole broadcast network or local station and that therefore profitability should be secondary to educating the public for the common good. But news professionals aren't usually as powerful as accountants. The idea is to make as much money as possible from news departments, sometimes to the detriment of truth and journalism.

Every broadcaster tries to determine how much programs are worth to the advertiser. But since they cannot go around to every home to find out what everyone is watching, broadcasters depend on ratings systems to measure audiences. Companies that do the surveys such as Nielsen and Arbitron use so-called scientific samples to find out how many people are watching each show. In these samples, less than a few thousand people may represent a whole nation of viewers. And from time to time, the sample may be exactly representational. Not always, by a long shot. In one case, a blind man living in the Bridgeport, Connecticut, area was representing a hundred thousand people. He enjoyed listening to television; the shows with the most interesting sound track got his vote.

Rating companies do not simply count the viewers of a particular show. As we mentioned earlier, they slice, dice, chop, and crunch the viewer information, then report to advertisers who pay them for these statistics. They try to know the age of those watching a specific show, their income, their level of education, what kinds of cars they own, what appliances they've bought, their eating habits, etc. The answers are produced by asking a sample of viewers questions either over the phone or in writing, and from logs that the viewers fill out. At least one rating service is experimenting with a device that would sit near the TV set and scan the room electronically to "see" how

many people are watching. The scanner would even identify the viewers.

What all of this means is that while you are watching
the TV set, you are being statistically watched, and very
carefully, by managers, accountants, and business people. They argue that they must know who you are to
mirror your interests and give you what you want. And
to pay for it they must run commercials. They also point
out that other news media—newspapers, for example—
are money-making enterprises and rely just as heavily
on advertising as does television. These arguments make
perfect sense in a free-enterprise business with no social
responsibility. But we would stress that broadcasting is
not just another business enterprise. Broadcasting is a
government-licensed activity using publicly owned airwaves and public facilities, and therefore, broadcasters
have an obligation not only to make money but to en-
lighten the public by supplying news and programs of
serious content for all segments of the population. To
this the TV establishment replies that television is the
most democratic institution in America. Every week a
plebiscite of sorts is held to determine which programs
are popular and which are not. The popular ones stay,
the others go. This proves, the accountants say, that our
programs give the public what it wants.

Serious journalists and social critics have an answer,
at least so far as news is concerned. It is this: when
providing the public with entertainment, the public's
preferences must be paramount. But news is different.

There are things the public must know whether or not they "like" it. To understand what is happening in the world and what it means requires knowledge of historical, political, and social contexts. It is the task of journalists to provide people with such knowledge. News is not entertainment. It is a necessity in a democratic society. Therefore, TV news must give people what they *need*, along with what they *want*. The solution is to present news in a form that will compel the attention of a large audience without subverting the goal of informing the public. But as things stand now, it is essential that any viewer understand the following when turning on a TV news show:

1. American television is an unsleeping money machine.
2. While journalists pursue newsworthy events, business-oriented management often makes decisions based on business considerations.
3. Many decisions about the form and content of news programs are made on the basis of information about the viewer, the purpose of which is to keep viewers watching so that they will be exposed to the commercials.

This is, obviously, not all that can be said about TV news, or else we could end our book here. But anything else that can, and will, be said must be understood within the framework of TV news as a commercial enterprise.

WHAT IS NEWS?

All this talk about news—what is it? We turn to this question because unless a television viewer has considered it, he or she is in danger of too easily accepting someone else's definition—for example, a definition supplied by the news director of a television station; or, even worse, a definition imposed by important advertisers. The question, in any case, is not a simple one and it is even possible that many journalists and advertisers have not thought deeply about it.

A simplistic definition of news can be drawn by paraphrasing Justice Oliver Wendell Holmes's famous definition of the law. The law, Holmes said, is what the courts say it is. Nothing more. Nothing less. In similar fashion, we might say that the news is what news directors and journalists say it is. In other words, when you turn on your television set to watch a network or local news show, whatever is on is, by definition, the news. But if we were to take that approach, on what basis would we say that we haven't been told enough? Or that a story that should have been covered wasn't? Or that too many stories of a certain type were included? Or that a reporter gave a flagrantly biased account?

If objections of this kind are raised by viewers, then they must have some conception of the news that the news show has not fulfilled. Most people, in fact, do have such a conception, although they are not always fully conscious of what it is. When people are asked "What is the news?" the most frequent answer given is that the news is "what happened that day." This is a rather silly answer since even those who give it can easily be made to see that an uncountable number of things happen during the course of a day, including what you had for breakfast, that could hardly be classified as news by any definition. In modifying their answer, most will add that the news is "important and interesting things that happened that day." This helps a little but leaves open the question of what is "important and interesting" and how that is decided. Embedded somewhere in one's understanding of the phrase "important and interesting events" is one's definition of "the news."

Of course, some people will say that the question of what is important and interesting is not in the least problematic. What the President says or does is important;

wars are important, rebellions, employment figures, elections, appointments to the Supreme Court. Really? We
doubt that even the President believes everything he says
is important. (Let us take, for example, President Bush's
remark that he doesn't like broccoli.) There are, as we
write, more than forty wars and rebellions going on somewhere in the world. Not even *The New York Times*, which
claims to be the "newspaper of public record," reports
on all of them, or even most. Are elections important?
Maybe. But we doubt you'd be interested in the election
in Iowa's Third Congressional District—unless you happen to live there. Some readers will remember the famous
comedy routine of the 2,000-Year-Old Man who was
discovered in the imaginations of Carl Reiner and Mel
Brooks. Upon being asked what he believed to be the
greatest invention of humankind during his life span, the
2,000-Year-Old Man replied unhesitatingly, "Saran
Wrap." Now, there is a great deal to be said for Saran
Wrap. We suspect that in the long run it may prove more
useful to the well-being of most of us than a number of
inventions that are daily given widespread publicity in
the news media. Yet it is fair to say that no one except
its manufacturer knows the date of Saran Wrap's invention, or even cares much to know. Saran Wrap is not
news. The color of Liz Taylor's wrap is. Or so some people
believe.

On the day Marilyn Monroe committed suicide, so
did many other people, some of whose reasons may have
been as engrossing as, and perhaps more significant than,

Miss Monroe's. But we shall never know about these people or their reasons; the journalists at CBS or NBC or *The New York Times* simply took no notice of them. Several people, we are sure, also committed suicide on the very day in 1991 when the New York Giants won the Super Bowl. We shall never learn about these people either, however instructive or interesting their stories may have been.

What we are driving at is this: "importance" is a judgment people make. Of course, there are some events—the assassination of a president, an earthquake, etc.—that have near-universal interest and consequences. But most news does not inhere in the event. An event *becomes* news. And it becomes news because it is selected for notice out of the buzzing, booming confusion around us. This may seem a fairly obvious point but keep in mind that many people believe that the news is always "out there," waiting to be gathered or collected. In fact, the news is more often *made* rather than gathered. And it is made on the basis of what the journalist thinks important or what the journalist thinks the audience thinks is important or interesting. It can get pretty complicated. Is a story about a killing in Northern Ireland more important than one about a killing in Morocco? The journalist might not think so but the audience might. Which story will become the news? And once selected, what point of view and details are to be included? After all, once a journalist has chosen an event to be news, he or she must also choose what is worth seeing, what is worth neglecting, and what is worth remembering or forgetting. This is simply another way of saying that every news story is a reflection of the reporter who tells the story. The reporter's previous assumptions about what is "out there" edit what he or she thinks is there. For example, many journalists believe that what is called "the intifada" is newsworthy. Let us suppose that a fourteen-year-old Palestinian boy hurls a Molotov cocktail at two eighteen-year-old Israeli soldiers. The explosion knocks one of the soldiers down and damages his left eye. The other soldier, terrified, fires a shot at the Palestinian that kills him instantly. The injured soldier eventually loses the sight of his eye. What details should be included in reporting this event? Is the age of the Palestinian relevant? Are the ages of the Israeli soldiers relevant? Is the injury to the soldier relevant? Was the act of the Palestinian provoked by the mere presence of Israeli soldiers? Was the act therefore justified? Is the shooting justified? Is the state of mind of the shooter relevant?

The answers to all of these questions, as well as to other questions about the event, depend entirely on the point of view of the journalist. You might think this is an exaggeration, that reporters, irrespective of their assumptions, can at least get the facts straight. But what are "facts"? In A. J. Liebling's book *The Press*, he gives a classic example of the problematic nature of "facts." On the same day, some years ago, both the *Wall Street Journal* and the now-defunct *World Telegram and Sun* featured a story about the streets of Moscow. Here is what the *Wall Street Journal* reporter wrote:

> The streets of central Moscow are, as the guide-books say, clean and neat; so is the famed sub-way. They are so because of an army of women with brooms, pans, and carts who thus earn their 35 rubles a month in lieu of "relief"; in all Moscow we never saw a mechanical street-sweeper.

Here is what the *World Telegram and Sun* reporter wrote:

> Four years ago [in Moscow] women by the hundreds swept big city streets. Now you rarely see more than a dozen. The streets are kept clean with giant brushing and sprinkling ma-chines.

Well, which is it? Can a dozen women look like an army? Are there giant machines cleaning the streets of Moscow or are there not? How can two trained journalists see events so differently? Well, one of them worked for the *Wall Street Journal*, and when these stories were written, it was the policy of the *Journal* to highlight the contrast between the primitive Russian economy and the sophisticated American economy. (It still is.) Does this mean the reporter for the *Journal* was lying? We doubt it. Each of our senses is a remarkably astute censor. We see what we expect to see; often, we focus on what we are paid to see. And those who pay us to see usually expect us to accept their notions not only of what is important but of what are important details.

That fact poses some difficult problems for those of us trying to make sense of the news we are given. One of these problems is indicated by a proposal, made years ago, by the great French writer Albert Camus. Camus wished to establish "a control newspaper." The newspaper would come out one hour after all the others and would contain estimates of the percentage of truth in each of their stories. In Camus's words: "We'd have complete dossiers on the interests, policies, and idiosyncrasies of the owners. Then we'd have a dossier on every journalist in the world. The interests, prejudices, and quirks of the owner would equal Z. The prejudices, quirks, and private interests of the journalist Y. Z times Y would give you X, the probable amount of truth in the story" (quoted in *The Press* by A. J. Liebling, p. 22n).

Camus was either a reckless mathematician or else he simply neglected to say why and how multiplying Z and Y would tell us what we need to know. (Why not add or divide them?) Nor did he discuss the problem of how to estimate the reliability of those doing the estimating. In any case, Camus died before he had a chance to publish such a newspaper, leaving each one of us to be our own "control center." Nonetheless, we can't help thinking how Camus's idea might be applied to television. Imagine how informative it would be if there were a five-minute television program that went on immediately after each television news show. The host might say something like this: "To begin with, this station is owned by Gary Farnsworth, who is also the president of Bontel Limited, the principal stockholder of which is the Sultan of Bahrain. Bontel Limited owns three Japanese electronic companies, two oil companies, the entire country of Upper Volta, and the western part of Romania. The anchorman on the television show earns $800,000 a year; his portfolio includes holdings in a major computer firm. He has a bachelor's degree in journalism from the University of Arkansas but was a C+ student, has never taken a course in political science, and speaks no language other than English. Last year, he read only two books—a biography of Cary Grant and a book of popular psychology called *Why Am I So Wonderful?* The reporter who covered the story on Yugoslavia speaks Serbo-Croatian, has a degree in international relations, and has had a Neiman Fellowship at Harvard University."

We think this kind of information would be helpful to a viewer although not for the same reason Camus did. Such information would not give an estimate of the "truth probability" of stories but it would suggest possible patterns of influence reflected in the news. After all, what is important to a person whose boss owns several oil companies might not be important to a person who doesn't even have a boss, who is unemployed. Similarly, what a reporter who does not know the language of the people he or she reports on can see and understand will probably be different from the perceptions of another reporter who knows the language well.

What we are saying is that to answer the question "What is news?" a viewer must know something about the political beliefs and economic situation of those who provide the news. The viewer is then in a position to know why certain events are considered important by those in charge of television news and may compare those judgments with his or her own.

But here's another problem. As we have implied, even oil magnates and poorly prepared jounalists do not consult, exclusively, their own interests in selecting the "truths" they will tell. Since they want people to watch their shows, they also try to determine what audiences think is important and interesting. There is, in fact, a point of view that argues against journalists imposing their own sense of significance on an audience. In this view, television news should consist only of those events that would interest the audience. The journalists must keep their own opinions to themselves. The response to this is that many viewers depend on journalists to advise them of what is important. Besides, even if journalists were mere followers of public interest, not all members of the audience agree on what they wish to know. For example, we do not happen to think that Liz Taylor's adventures in marriage were or are of any importance whatsoever to anyone but her and Michael Wilding, Nicky Hilton, Mike Todd, Eddie Fisher, Richard Burton, John Warner, Larry Fortensky, and, of course, Debbie

Reynolds and Sybil Burton. Obviously, most people don't agree, which is why an announcement of her intention to marry again is featured on every television news show. What's our point? A viewer must not only know what he or she thinks is significant but what others believe is significant as well.

It is a matter to be seriously considered. You may conclude, for example, that other people do not have a profound conception of what is significant. You may even be contemptuous of the taste or interests of others. On the other hand, you may fully share the sense of significance held by a majority of people. It is not our purpose here to instruct you or anyone else in what is to be regarded as a significant event. We are saying that in considering the question "What is news?" a viewer must always take into account his or her relationship to a larger audience. Television is a mass medium, which means that a television news show is not intended for you alone. It is public communication, and the viewer needs to have some knowledge and opinions about "the public." It is a common complaint of individuals that television news rarely includes stories about some part of the world in which those individuals have some special interest. We know a man, for example, who emigrated from Switzerland thirty years ago. He is an American citizen but retains a lively interest in his native land. "Why," he asked us, "are there never any stories about Switzerland?" "Because," we had to reply, "no one but you and a few others have any interest in Switzerland." "That's too bad," he replied. "Switzerland is an interesting country." We agree. But most Americans have not been in Switzerland, probably believe not much happens in Switzerland, do not have many relatives in Switzerland, and would much rather know about what some English lord has to say about the world's economy than what a Swiss banker thinks. Maybe they are right, maybe not. Judging the public mind is always risky.

And this leads to another difficulty in answering the question "What is news?" Some might agree with us that Liz Taylor's adventures in marriage do not constitute significant events but that they ought to be included in a news show precisely for that reason. Her experiences, they may say, are amusing or diverting, certainly engrossing. In other words, the purpose of news should be to give people pleasure, at least to the extent that it takes their minds off their own troubles. We have heard people say that getting through the day is difficult enough, filled with tension, anxiety, and often disappointment. When they turn on the news, they want relief, not aggravation. It is also said that whether entertaining or not, stories about the lives of celebrities should be included because they are instructive; they reveal a great deal about our society—its mores, values, ideals. Mark Twain once remarked that news is history in its first and best form. The American poet Ezra Pound added an interesting idea to that. He defined literature as news that *stays* news. Among other things, Pound meant that the stuff of literature originates not in stories about the World Bank or an armistice agreement but in those simple, repeatable tales that reflect the pain, confusion, or exaltations that are constant in human experience, and touch us at the deepest levels. For example, consider the death of Michael Landon. Who was Michael Landon to you, or you to Michael Landon that you should have been told so much about him when he died? Here is a possible answer: Michael Landon was rich, decent, handsome, young, and successful. Suddenly, very nearly without warning, he was struck down at the height of his powers and fame. Why? What are we to make of it? Why him? It is like some Old Testament parable; these questions were raised five thousand years ago and we still raise them today. It is the kind of story that *stays* news, and that is why it must be given prominence. Or so some people believe.

What about the kind of news that doesn't stay news, that is neither the stuff of history nor literature—the fires, rapes, and murders that are daily featured on local television news? Who has decided that they are important, and why? One cynical answer is that they are there because viewers take comfort in the realization that *they* have escaped disaster. At least for that day. It doesn't matter who in particular was murdered; the viewer wasn't. We tune in to find out how lucky we are, and go to sleep with the pleasure of knowing that we have survived. A somewhat different answer goes this way: it is the task of the news show to provide a daily accounting of the progress of society. This can be done in many ways, some of them abstract (for example, a report on the state of unemployment), some of them concrete (for example, reports on particularly gruesome murders). These reports, especially those of a concrete nature, are the daily facts from which the audience is expected to draw appropriate conclusions about the question "What kind of society am I a member of?" Studies conducted by Professor George Gerbner and his associates at the University of Pennsylvania have shown that people who are heavy television viewers, including viewers of television news shows, believe their communities are much more dangerous than do light television viewers. Television news, in other words, tends to frighten people. The question is, "Ought they to be frightened?" which is to ask, "Is the news an accurate portrayal of where we are as a society?" Which leads to another question, "Is it possible for daily news to give such a picture?" Many journalists believe it is possible. Some are skeptical. The early-twentieth-century journalist Lincoln Steffens proved that he could create a "crime wave" anytime he wanted by simply writing about all the crimes that normally occur in a large city during the course of a month. He could also end the crime wave by not writing about them. If crime waves can be "manufactured" by journalists, then how accurate are news shows in depicting the condition of a society? Besides, murders, rapes, and fires (even unemployment figures) are not the only way to assess the progress (or regress) of a society. Why are there so few television stories about symphonies that have been composed, novels written, scientific problems solved, and a thousand other creative acts that occur during the course of a month? Were television news to be filled with these events, we would not be frightened. We would, in fact, be inspired, optimistic, cheerful.

One answer is as follows: these events make poor television news because there is so little to show about them. In the judgment of most editors, people *watch* television. And what they are interested in watching are exciting, intriguing, even exotic pictures. Suppose a scientist has developed a new theory about how to measure with more exactitude the speed with which heavenly objects are moving away from the earth. It is difficult to televise a theory, especially it if involves complex mathematics. You can show the scientist talking about his theory but that would not make for good television and too much of it would drive viewers to other stations. In any case, the news show could only give the scientist twenty seconds of air time because time is an important commodity. Newspapers and magazines sell space, which is not without its limitations for a commercial enterprise. But space can be expanded. Television sells time, and time cannot be expanded. This means that whatever else is neglected, commercials cannot be. Which leads to another possible answer to the question "What is news?" News, we might say, may be history in its first and best form, or the stuff of literature, or a record of the condition of a society, or the expression of the passions of a public, or the prejudices of journalists. It may be all of these things but in its worst form it can also be mainly a "filler," a "come-on" to keep the viewer's attention until the commercials come. Certain producers have learned that by pandering to the audience, by eschewing solid news and replacing it with leering sensationalism, they can subvert the news by presenting a "television commercial show" that is interrupted by news.

All of which leads us to reiterate, first, that there are no simple answers to the question "What is news?" and second, that it is not our purpose to tell you what you ought to believe about the question. The purpose of this chapter is to arouse your interest in thinking *about* the question. Your answers are to be found by knowing what you feel is significant and how your sense of the significant conforms with or departs from that of others, including broadcasters, their bosses, and their audiences. Answers are to be found in your ideas about the purposes of public communication, and in your judgment of the kind of society you live in and wish to live in. We cannot provide answers to these questions. But you also need to know something about the problems, limitations, traditions, motivations, and, yes, even the delusions of the television news industry. That's where we can help you to know how to watch a television news show.

3

Getting Them into the Electronic Tent

At carnival sideshows, the barkers used to shout intriguing things to attract an audience. "Step right up. For one thin dime, see what men have died for and others lusted after. The Dance of the Veils as only Tanya can do it." The crowd would gather as lovely Tanya, wrapped in diaphanous garb, would wiggle a bit, and entice grown men who should have known better to part with their money for a ticket. Instead of seeing Tanya shed her clothes, her customers only shed their money.

In television news there is no Tanya we know of but there are plenty of Sonyas, Marias, Ricks, and Brads who have the job of getting you into the electronic tent. They come on the air and try to intrigue you with come-ons to get you to watch their show. "Step right up" becomes

"Coming up at eleven o'clock." And, instead of veils, you get a glimpse of some videotape which may intrigue you enough to part with your time instead of a dime. It is no accident that in the television news industry, the short blurb aimed at getting you to watch a program is called a "tease." Sometimes it delivers what it advertises but often it hooks us into the electronic tent and keeps us there long enough that we don't remember why we were there in the first place.

The tease is designed to be very effective, very quickly. By definition, a tease lasts about ten seconds or less and the information it contains works like a headline. Its purpose is to grab your attention and keep you watching. In the blink of a tease you are enticed to stay tuned with promises of exclusive stories and tape, good-looking anchors, helicopters, team coverage, hidden cameras, uniform blazers, and even, yes, better journalism. It is all designed to stop you from using the remote-control button to switch channels. But the teasing doesn't stop there. During each news program, just before each commercial, you will see what are known as "bumpers"— teases that are aimed at keeping you in the tent, keeping you from straying to another channel where other wonders are being touted. And the electronic temptations do not even cease with the end of the program. When the news show is over, you are still being pleaded with "not to turn that dial" so that you can tune in the next day for an early-morning newscast, which in turn will suggest you watch the next news program and so on. If news programmers had it their way, you would watch a steady diet of news programs, one hooking you into the next with only slight moments of relief during station breaks.

If you think you can beat the system by not watching teases, you'll need to think again. We are dealing here with serious professional hucksters. The game plan, aimed at getting you to watch the news, starts even before you have seen the first tease. It starts while you're watching the entertainment shows *before* the news. Whether you know it or not, we are programmed to watch the news, by programmers. They know that most of us tend to be lazy. Even with remote controls at our fingertips, we are likely to stay tuned to the channel we have been watching. So the United Couch Potatoes of America sit and sit, and sit, and before they know it, Marsha and Rick have hooked us into their news program, promising "team coverage," no less, of today's latest disaster. In the textbook vernacular: the lead-in programs must leave a residual audience for the news shows which follow. To put it plainly, a station with a strong lineup of entertainment programs can attract a large audience to the news tent. High-rated shows such as "Oprah Winfrey," programmed just before the news, bring in a big audience and premium prices at the broadcast marketplace. This is why the best news program may not have ratings as high as a news program with a strong lead-in. It may not be fair but it is television.

Now, let us say all things are equal. Station A and station B both have excellent lead-ins. What news program will you watch? Most people will say something like "I want the latest news, the best reporting with state-of-the-art technology presented by people I can trust and respect."

But while people might say they like the most experienced journalists presenting the news, many news consultants claim that no matter what they *say*, the audience prefers to watch good-looking, likable people it can relate to (perhaps of the same age group, race, etc.). News organizations spend a lot of time and money building up the reputations of their anchors, sending them to high-visibility stories that they hope will convince viewers that they are watching top-level journalists. Unfortunately, in some markets the top anchors are sometimes "hat racks" who read beautifully but who can barely type a sentence or two without the aid of a producer and writer. They may know how to anchor but many are strictly lightweights. In television, looking the part is better than being the real item, a situation you would rightly reject in other contexts. Imagine going to a doctor who hadn't studied medicine, but rather looks like a doctor —authoritative, kindly, understanding, and surrounded by formidable machinery. We assume you would reject such a professional fraud especially if he or she had majored in theater arts in college. But this kind of play-acting is perfectly acceptable in the world of television news and entertainment where actors who have played lawyers on a TV series frequently are called on to give speeches at lawyers' conventions and men who have played doctors are invited to speak at gatherings of medical professionals. If you can read news convincingly on television, you can have a successful career as an anchor, no journalism experience required. This is not to say there aren't bright men and women who are knowledgeable journalists and who can and do serve as anchors. But the problem is that it is almost impossible for the viewer to figure out which anchor knows his stuff and who's faking it. A good anchor is a good actor and with the lift of an eyebrow or with studied seriousness of visage, he or she can convince you that you are seeing the real thing, that is, a concerned, solid journalist.

You may wonder at this point, what difference does it make? Even if one cannot distinguish an experienced journalist from a good actor playing the part of an experienced journalist, wouldn't the news be the same? Not quite. An experienced journalist is likely to have a sense of what is particularly relevant about a story and insist on including certain facts and a perspective that the actor-anchor would have no knowledge of. Of course, it is true that often an experienced journalist, working behind the cameras, has prepared the script for the actor-anchor. But when the anchor is himself or herself a journalist, the story is likely to be given additional dimensions, especially if the journalist-anchor does his or her own script writing.

And there is one more point: even if there were no differences between the stories presented by actor-anchors and journalist-anchors, the fact that the audience is being deluded into thinking that an actor-anchor is a journalist contributes a note of fakery to the enterprise. It encourages producers and news directors to think about what they are doing as artifice, as a show in which truth-telling is less important than the appearance of truth-telling. One can hardly blame them. They know that everything depends on their winning the audience's favor, and the anchor is the key weapon in their arsenal.

If you are skeptical about the importance of the anchor in attracting the audience to the electronic tent, you must ask yourself why they are paid so much. Network anchors earn over a million dollars a year. Over two million dollars a year. Do we hear three? Yes, more than three million dollars a year in the case of Dan Rather at CBS. Is he worth it? From a financial point of view, certainly. He brings people into the tent because they perceive him to be an experienced, solid reporter, who has paid his dues and knows what's going on. And an experienced newsman such as Rather starts to look like a bargain when you think of local anchors being paid as much as 750,000 to a million dollars without serious journalistic credentials. Anchors who work for network-affiliated stations in the top ten markets make an average of $139,447 a year. Nationwide, the average anchor, as of this writing, makes $52,284 a year, according to the National Association of Broadcasters.

So there you are ready to watch the news presented by a high-priced anchor and on comes the show, complete with a fancy opening, and music sounding as though it was composed for a Hollywood epic. The host appears —an anchor god or goddess sculpted on Mount Arbitron, at least the best of them. But even the worst looks authoritative. Of course, the anchor has had plenty of help from plenty of crafts people in creating the illusion of calm omniscience. After all, it's not all hair spray. That glittering, well-coiffed, Commanding Presence has been placed in a setting that has been designed, built, and painted to make him or her look as wonderful as possible. Consultants have been used to make sure the lights are fine-tuned to highlight the hair and to fill in wrinkles. Color experts have complemented the star's complexion with favorable background hues. Short anchors have their seats raised to look taller, with makeup applied to create just the right look, accenting cheekbones, covering baldness, enlarging small eyes, hiding blemishes, perhaps obscuring a double chin.

And of course there is camera magic. A low camera angle can make a slight anchor look imposing. Long and medium shots, rather than close-ups, can hide bags under the eyes. The anchor-star has probably had the benefit of a clothing allowance and the best hairdressers and consultants. It is cosmetic television at its finest.

The music fades and the parade of stories and the people reporting them begins. Whom you see depends sometimes on professional competence and journalistic ability. But it may also depend on the results of "focus groups," where ordinary viewers are shown videotapes and are then asked which anchors and reporters they prefer to watch and why. The group gives its opinion without the benefit of observing a performer over a period of time or knowledge of the reporter's background and experience. What is wanted is an immediate, largely emotional reaction. Performers are also evaluated by a service called "TV Q," which claims to rate television performers on the basis of who the public recognizes. The company, called Marketing Evaluations/TV Q, polls about six thousand Americans by mail, then sells the results to networks, advertising agencies, and anyone else willing to spend about a thousand dollars to find out someone's Q score.

Some news show consultants believe in forming a television news pseudo-family to attract audiences. After the "Today" show started to slide in the ratings, NBC brought back sportscaster Joe Garagiola to try to pep up the ratings. Garagiola had been on the program from 1969 to 1973. NBC had alienated its viewers by replacing popular coanchor Jane Pauley with Deborah Norville, who was supposed to be a hot ratings-getter. She wasn't. The show nosedived. Executives realized they needed something or somebody with pizazz. They reached for a person who, they hoped, could make the "Today" show cast a family again. Warm, affable Joe Garagiola. The return of the Prodigal Son. Exit Norville, now cast as the "other woman."

The "family" concept is at work at many local stations. The anchors probably will be a couple, male and female, both good-looking and in the same relative age category as husband-wife (although in our modern society with second marriages common, the male anchor may be twenty years older than his female counterpart). The other "family" members may be like Archie and Veronica to appeal to the younger set: Archie the sportscaster, who never tires of watching videotapes of highlights and bloopers, and Veronica the weather person. There is also Mr. or Ms. Breathless Showbiz who always feigns being thrilled to see the heartthrob or hottest rock group of the moment.

Whatever kind of television family is presented, it always has one thing in common. It is a happy family, where everybody gets along with everyone else (at least for thirty minutes) and knows his or her place. The viewer usually gets to see the whole "family" at the "top," or beginning, of the show. They will either be featured in a taped introduction or be sitting on the set, en masse, to create a sense of cohesion and stability. Throughout the program, members of the family will come on the set and do their turn, depending on their specialty. No newscast is complete without Archie the Sportscaster rattling off a list of clichés that he believes bond him to his fans. "Yes!" "In your face!" "Let's go to the videotape!" "Swish!"

Theoretically, sportscasters are supposed to be reporters, not fans. But depending on what they believe to be the roots of their popularity they might decide to bask in the glorious light of sports heroes and become cheerleaders. It is, in any event, the sportscaster's job to keep the audience excited, complete with taped highlights and interviews with the top players who often have nothing more to contribute than standard-brand sports-hero remarks: "It's not important how I played, as long as I can contribute to the team" or "I might have scored a few more touchdowns, but the real credit has to go to the front line who made it all possible." Picture and cliché blend to fill the eye with a sense of action and the nose with the macho smell of the locker room.

No newscast would be complete without a weather report that usually starts with a review of what already happened that day. The report is supposedly made interesting by moving H's and L's, and by making clouds and isobars stalk across a map. Whatever the weather, the one thing you can always count on is a commercial break *before* tomorrow's weather forecast. You can also count on the peculiar tendency of anchors to endow the weather person with God-like meteorological power as in, "Well, Veronica, I hope you'll bring us some relief from this rain." To which the reply is something like "Oh, Chuck, I'm afraid we've got some more rain coming tomorrow, but wait till you see what I've got for you this weekend."

If you have ever wondered why all this fuss is made about the weather, the answer is that, for reasons no one knows, weather information is of almost universal interest. This means that it usually attracts an attentive audience, which in turn means it provides a good environment for commercials. The executive producer of the

"CBS This Morning" show, Eric Sorensen, has remarked that research shows weather news is the most important reason why people watch TV in the morning. The weather segments also give the anchors a chance to banter with the weather people and lighten the proceedings. A pleasing personality is almost certainly more important to a weathercaster than a degree in meteorology. How significant personality is can be gauged by what these people earn. Weather people in small markets earn an average of $21,980 a year, according to the National Association of Broadcasters. Weathercasters make an average of $86,589 in the top ten markets, with some earning a half million dollars or more. Nonetheless, it should not surprise you to know that these people rarely prepare weather forecasts. There are staff meteorologists for that. The on-air weather person is expected to draw audiences, not weather maps.

Feature reporters usually ply their craft near the "back of the book," close by the weather. They keep the mood light, and try to leave the viewer with a smile. The subject matter of some feature vignettes is called "evergreen" because it is not supposed to wilt with the passage of time. It can be stored until needed. (Two of the best practitioners of "evergreen art" are Charles Kuralt and Andy Rooney.) Locally, you usually see "evergreen" reports on slow news days, when the editor has trouble filling the news budget (the newsworthy events of the day). But as entertaining news becomes more of a commodity, feature reports are being used more and more to attract and hold audiences through the news program.

No news "family" would be complete without a science reporter, a Doctor Wizard, who usually wears glasses, may have an advanced degree, and is certainly gray around the temples. These experts bring to the audience the latest in everything from cancer research to the designer disease of the year.

Once the family has gathered, everyone in place, each with a specific role, the show is ready to begin. The anchor reads the lead story. If you are expecting to hear the most important news to you, on any given day, you will often be disappointed. Never forget that the producer of the program is trying to grab you before you zap away to another news show. Therefore, chances are you will hear a story such as Zsa Zsa's run-in with the law, Rob Lowe's home videos, Royal Family happenings, or news of a Michael Jackson tour. Those stories have glitter and glamour in today's journalism. And if glitter and glamour won't do the job, gore will. Body bags have become an important currency of TV news and a four-bagger is a grand slam.

If viewers have stayed through the lead story, they probably will be hooked for a while because the newscast is designed to keep their attention through the commercial breaks into the next "section," when the process starts again. Taped stories from reporters are peppered throughout the show to keep interest from flagging as anchors keep the show on track "eyeballing," or reading, stories on camera. When the news stories thin out, there are sports, features, and weather to fill up the time.

All this is presented with slick lighting and production values, moving along at a crisp pace. The tempo is usually fast since some programmers believe that fast-paced news programs attract younger audiences. Older audiences, they believe, are attracted to a slower-paced, quieter presentation. No matter how fast or slow the pace of the show, there is not much time to present anything but truncated information. After we have subtracted commercial time, about twenty-two minutes of editorial time are available in a half-hour broadcast. If we subtract, further, the time used for introductions, closings, sports, and the weather, we are left with about fifteen minutes. If there are five taped stories of two minutes each, that leaves five or six minutes to cover the rest of the world's events. And if more time is subtracted for "happy talk," chalk up another minute or so just for "schmoozing" on the set.

Given the limited time and objectives of a television newscast, a viewer has to realize that he or she is not getting a full meal but rather a snack. And depending on the organization presenting the news, the meal may contain plenty of empty calories.

4

Donuts,
Big Foot, Mules,
and the
Bird

Up to this point, we have taken what some might regard as a cynical perspective on TV news. We think we have been more realistic than cynical. And we wish to continue to be realistic. Which means that although the competitive news wars are fought by anchor-personalities, there are others who are indispensable to the victories. As in real wars, the spectacular heroes always get the headlines, but it is the foot soldiers who win the battles by grinding out the victories day by day, inch by inch. In the TV wars, the foot soldiers are the general-assignment reporters who crank out stories, frame by frame, whether the amount of news is a flood or a trickle. In the trade they are known as "mules" because they work long hours, travel far, and carry the burden of getting and presenting stories of significant substance, even if such stories are neither glamorous nor intriguing.

If the mule works well out in the field, he or she may be promoted to the status of a "big foot." A big foot is a reporter who is sent to the major stories that are sure to attract attention and may be the lead stories on any particular show. The big feet are star reporters and often earn big dollars, although never as much as a star anchor. Big feet may even have their own staffs, including a field producer. Dr. Joe Foote (whose name only coincidentally calls to mind his scholarly interest) of Southern Illinois University has kept an eye on big feet and has concluded that any network correspondent picked to cover the "iron triangle" of the White House, the Pentagon, and the State Department, or anyone involved in coverage of a presidential election, has career success guaranteed.

At contract-negotiation time, a big foot may demand prominent display on the air, special perks including clothing allowances, jobs for assistants, and, in one case we know of, even her own hairdresser. In return, he or she is expected to pick up at a moment's notice and travel just about anywhere news is breaking. And they are absolutely expected to get their story on the air that night. The best among them can earn between $100,000 and $200,000 a year even at a local level in the large markets. In smaller cities, of course, they may make much less.

The average news reporter working for the average television station in the United States makes about $25,000 a year. In the smallest markets the average pay is $15,912 for reporters. In the top ten markets (New York, Los Angeles, Chicago, San Francisco, Philadelphia, Detroit, Boston, Dallas, Washington, D.C., and Houston), they earned $60,268 a year. Network reporting stars may earn between $100,000 and a million dollars (if they are prominently featured on a show).

But don't dash out to buy a trench coat and hair spray for your new career as a correspondent until you hear about some of the drawbacks. For openers, there are the long hours. You may see a reporter doing a stand-up on the screen for just a few seconds but it may have taken ten hours to get the story and the pictures to match. Think about it. On radio, a reporter could say, "The camels came over the Alps carrying food and guns, as a fierce storm lashed the animals and their masters with hard hailstones." It might take a few minutes to write that script or a few moments to ad-lib it. But the same scene on television is a camel with a different hump. Imagine how difficult it would be to videotape the pictures to match that description. And if the event happened at night on a steep bit of terrain, it would be even more difficult to record on tape. On television, reporters may have to drive miles or wait on a stakeout for hours just to get a simple shot that will last five or ten seconds on the screen. It's hard work. Many reporters get to work at eight in the morning. They may be sent to the courthouse, to a fire or a crane collapse, depending on what is happening that day. Let's say a reporter is assigned coverage of an important trial. If she is in the right position, at the entrance the defendants use, she may get pictures and manage to shout a quick question before the court convenes. Leaving the camera crew in position, the reporter dashes to the courtroom to cover the case and tries to absorb the more esoteric points of law. She may talk with attorneys and other observers during the breaks to gain further insights. At the end of the daily court session the reporter must then decide what tape, if any, to use; she may want to shoot the work of courtroom artists, if any; she'll have to line up on-camera interviews, write a comprehensive and easily understandable script, learn it, and be prepared to go on the air live, while giving the impression she is in total control of the situation. Having done that for the early news, the reporter may be asked by the producer to provide a live presence at the courthouse for the late news. The reporter may watch the fifteenth hour slip by before being able to get home, fall into bed, and dream of torts and rules of evidence before starting over again the next day.

Not too long ago, the reporter had to wait for film to be developed before a visual story could be presented on the air. Now, videotape provides instant pictures, which solves the problem of processing delays. But the newfound speed has caused other problems. For example, the audience expects to see events on the tube quickly if not live. With the advent of satellite technology, a reporter may fly to the scene of a story, dig to get the information and pictures she needs, then file a series of individually tailored reports for several stations, each having a specific need. If the stations are in different time zones, the work can be grueling, albeit with high visibility and pay.

Years ago, if there was major news, the public might see pictures of the event in their movie theaters a week or so later. But since we now expect to see live pictures from the scene almost immediately on TV, a new dimension has been added to the news-show wars. News departments compete with one another to be first in delivering the pictures. Each network usually budgets between $200,000 and $300,000 a month for special-event coverage, three or four million dollars a year. But when many major international stories happen, all stops are pulled out. Events such as the invasion of Panama can cost a network two million dollars to cover. A similar amount was spent by each network to report from China on the rebellion, and roughly the same amount to cover the coup in the Soviet Union. Television stations are fierce in their desire to get a picture from the scene on the air first. On the plus side, we get to see the view from the camera's eye, quickly and relatively unfettered. But there is a price we pay for supersonic journalism: the historic function of journalism is either forgotten or distorted. In the frantic quest to be first with film footage or even a "fast-breaking" story that is not accompanied by pictures, TV news departments do not have the time, resources, or the interest to explain the meaning of the event. Journalism is supposed to present facts in an accurate and orderly fashion. It is also supposed to place the facts in some political or sociological context so that viewers have some sense of how to weigh the facts and what value to give to them.

About the only concession news departments make to this tradition is to call upon "political experts," usually a nervous-looking person from Georgetown University who is in the studio or his office. The anchor asks the expert if this story is important and what will happen from here. The expert answers by saying that the story is *very* important and only time will tell about the future. This charade takes about thirty seconds.

The real "experts" turn out to be the reporters racing to the scene of stories, often arriving just minutes before air time. What kinds of experts are they? Well, often they are filled in on story details from their assignment editors via mobile radios or cellular phones while they're en route to the scene. What this means is that TV reporters dash to the microphone with just a smattering of knowledge and bounce the slim reportage off a satellite to your home. While the image of an event hurtles through the air with enormous speed, the perspective that comes with thoughtful reflection is thrown to the wind, in favor of "now you see it . . . now you don't" journalism.

Of course, there are some experienced, talented reporters who can grasp stories quickly and report effectively on the run. And they will be more and more in demand for their ability to ad-lib and process information quickly as new technologies are developed to bring the news faster. But the average reporter is not able to keep up with "warp speed," and we will have to settle most of the time for reporting that has little substance, if any.

The competitive drive to get the story on the air quickly and the technological ability to do so obviously reduce the ability of journalists to check facts and other information. When the news is transmitted instantaneously, without the benefit of a gatekeeper or journalist to review it before airing, the result can be dramatic and at times false and misleading. For example, as reported by CBS and ABC news, in 1990, before the United States went to war against Iraq, a congressional caucus heard testimony supposedly from a Kuwaiti refugee telling of inhuman horror. The witness, Nayirah al-Sabah, told of watching Iraqi troops take babies out of incubators in a Kuwaiti hospital, put the babies on a cold floor to die, and remove the incubators, apparently for shipment to Iraq. The television picture was dramatic. The witness cried as she told her story, and the moving testimony, later quoted by President Bush in speeches, may have helped convince the American public and Congress to go to war against Iraq. But it has been revealed that the "eyewitness" was in reality the daughter of the Kuwaiti ambassador to the United States. It was further alleged that she had been coached by the public relations firm of Hill and Knowlton, whose client, Citizens for a Free

Kuwait, was primarily funded by the emir of Kuwait. According to Kuwaiti doctors interviewed by "20/20" and "60 Minutes," no such incidents had occurred.

One way local producers deal with the lighting speed of information transmission is to prepare some segments of live news events in advance. This is accomplished by preparing a "donut." A "donut" is material that has been taped, edited, and then presented after a live introduction. It is usually followed by a live "outro" by a reporter on camera in the field. Which is why, when you see a report on television, you usually hear the latest news from the reporter live on the scene, who then introduces older taped material, then brings you up to date live at the end of the report: a "donut."

What we are talking about here, and what is a constant obstacle in TV journalism, is the pressure of time. Time works against understanding, coherence, and even meaning. The practical needs of a show, especially getting on the air at a specific time, call for the reporter to do the best he can under the circumstances. The producer may also want a "live" stand-up at the scene of a story, requiring valuable travel time. Network affiliate stations frequently want "live" on-scene reports regardless of the difference in time zones. News producers operating from a distance and shielded from the difficulties in the field can make unnecessary and impractical demands. And the plethora of morning news and business shows can make certain stories round-the-clock assignments. The correspondent may be whipped in five directions at once and be expected to be well-informed and composed while presenting an in-depth report. All this, and a glamorous demeanor as well.

In fact, no matter how much effort, intelligence, and craft a television reporter may bring to a story, viewer mail will invariably bring comments about the reporter's appearance. A reporter can hang out of a helicopter, get great pictures, and tell a cohesive story, but that's not good enough for some viewers, who will complain that the reporter's hair was standing up. Some viewers will request the name of his tailor. That is why some reporters will go to greater lengths to look good than to get the full story. But news people not only dress to impress their viewers; they put on airs. Besides the clothing they wear, television journalists often wear titles. In these days of hyperbole, puffery, and imagery, a reporter even for the smallest station may be called a correspondent or, even better, a senior correspondent (whatever that is) simply because the news director gives him the label. Years ago, men and women who pounded the pavements reporting stories were called "reporters." A few exalted network icons were promoted to the rank of "correspondent" by virtue of experience, knowledge, and journalistic abilites. No more. Everyone is at least a correspondent.

Perhaps the glamorous names have something to do with the glamorous technologies that are now so much a part of the news industry. "Reporter" is a word associated with a pad and pencil, a portable typewriter, and an old-fashioned dial telephone. "Correspondent" suggests a new era. New times, some say, require new words. And these are certainly new times. Over the past decade, the way a reporter gets the job done has radically changed. The *Washington Journalism Review* gives one dramatic example told by CBS News associate producer David Hawthorne. He was on a flight leaving New York's La Guardia Airport for North Carolina on his way to cover Hurricane Hugo. The plane aborted the takeoff and crashed into the water. Hawthorne helped several mothers get their children out on the wing of the plane, then managed to climb back into the shattered fuselage to retrieve his cellular phone from under his seat. He immediately called CBS and from the crash site he was put on the air with Dan Rather for the first actual live report from the scene.

Not only professionals are taking advantage of new technology. Across the country, amateurs are using their lightweight, inexpensive camcorders to broaden news coverage. On October 17, 1989, Debbie Kelly was driving home to Oklahoma from a West Coast vacation when an earthquake struck northern California. As it happened, Debbie was on the San Francisco Bay Bridge when part of the bridge collapsed. She was able to shoot video pictures of one of the most famous shots of the catastrophe—a car plunging off the collapsed section of the bridge. George Holliday's videotape of the beating of Rodney King by Los Angeles policemen had enormous impact across the nation. With more people like George Holliday recording events on their camcorders, news directors are predicting widespread use of amateur videos on newscasts in the future.

Camcorders, cellular phones, and lap-top computers may be helpful but nothing has been more influential to television news reporting than the satellite, which allows television signals to be bounced from earth to space and back quickly and relatively inexpensively. In November of 1989, the Berlin Wall fell when the East German government allowed its citizens to travel to West Berlin. Hundreds of thousands of Germans gathered at the wall. So did hundreds of anchormen and women. Local TV viewers watched something that had been crumbling for some time—the illusion that only networks could bring the public news from the far corners of the earth. The launch of communications satellites, known in the TV business as "birds," resulted in local audiences getting a bird's-eye view of the world. The satellites are launched into a pattern 22,000 miles around the earth, in a geosynchronous orbit—that is, moving so that the satellite remains over the same spot on earth. In this way, signals can be sent to it and bounced back to earth stations for reception.

Once upon a time, NBC linked both coasts of the United States via coaxial cable, showing the Atlantic and Pacific at the same time on a split screen. It was an expensive technology requiring the laying of a thick cable from coast to coast, and to every television station receiving the signal. Now, local stations, which could not afford the expensive cost of sending television signals via earth cables, can afford to get a signal from just about anywhere on earth. All in the blink of the eye, about a half second.

With satellite technology it is now possible for a local station to pull in and present multiple pictures on the screen simultaneously. Local stations can put their anchors on a plane and put them on the air from the Wailing Wall, the walls of the Kremlin, the Berlin Wall, the Great Wall of China, or any other wall worthy of international notice. Supported by tape from sources including CNN, local news operations can now present their audiences with the same stories as the networks do.

In the not-so-distant future, technology will continue to change radically what we see and how we see it. The new buzz word in the network halls is "videojournalist," a reporter who carries a camera, shoots the story, and also reports it. This will require someone with more than good looks and charm, a person capable of operating a camera while narrating the scene. NBC News says it hopes to use more videojournalists and CBS News is reportedly training some of its staff for the job. There are those who predict that the networks will eventually close their worldwide bureaus and rely on "stringer" videojournalists. Can a journalist ferret out the facts while operating as a one-man band? Will the artistry of the picture suffer? No one knows yet. But there is no question that the advancing technology makes the videojournalist not only a possibility at the network level but an economic necessity. But economics are pushing major news organizations in other ways as well.

For almost fifty years the three networks dominated international news coverage not only because of their technological and financial resources but also because of their commitment to excellence. During World War II, Edward R. Murrow built the CBS News team, recruiting top-level print newsmen for radio. They helped invent broadcast news at its finest and that tradition was carried over to television. The other networks built their news departments of global depth and experience in a similar fashion. Many experienced journalists remained at the same network for most of their careers out of loyalty and commitment. But in the 1980s, with the three networks now run by corporate conglomerates, the commitment to the dollar replaced the commitment to excellence. News bureaus were cut back in personnel and budgets. Veteran reporters who had risked their lives in Vietnam and other danger spots were discharged—all this while a few well-known anchors and reporters demanded and received extravagant salaries. Former CBS News president Fred Friendly called the situation a "harvest of greed," a reference to the famous CBS documentary by Edward R. Murrow, "Harvest of Shame." Friendly told an "Ethics and Television" seminar that high-priced stars like Dan Rather and Diane Sawyer should voluntarily give up one-third of their salaries to save the jobs of hundreds of CBS employees cut back in a financial crunch in the late 1980s. Friendly remarked, "No journalist requires one or two or three million dollars a year." It is, he believes, "unhealthy, unacceptable, and unethical" for television journalists to make ten times more than the President of the United States and twenty times more than members of Congress. Friendly made no allies among the superstar news personalities by adding, "For these talented and dedicated journalists . . . to stand idly, while the important foundations of the best and most comprehensive team in broadcasting journalism anywhere begins to crumble, approaches an exercise in unethical behavior."

Friendly's reproaches notwithstanding, reporters and other news talent took note of the new corporate climate and many sold their services to the highest bidder. In effect, the networks became homogenized as anchors and reporters switched call letters. NBC's Connie Chung found a new home at CBS at a million dollars a year. CBS's Diane Sawyer moved to ABC for a reported $1.6 million a year. Chris Wallace switched channels, for exactly how much we have not been told. As defection followed defection, the unique elements that once defined each network disappeared. Behind the scenes, news producers and writers also switched allegiances and jobs. Network news shows began looking and sounding alike, leading with similar stories, often featuring reporters and anchors who had formerly worked for the competition. Indeed, following the war in the Persian Gulf where "pool" reporting was the norm, the networks decided to try to "pool" certain coverage at the White House and some trips by the President. In 1991 CBS News and Ted Turner's Cable News Network decided to share a news bureau in Berlin. While the two networks kept separate editorial staffs of correspondents and producers, they decided to use the same office facilities and technical operations including satellite equipment. They estimated the shared arrangement would save a total of $400,000 a year. Apparently the savings in costs are greater than the need to function as an independent news source. Nowadays, the mix-and-match network operations often are separated in the ratings by just fractions of a point, as they all serve up similar fare.

In local news, the battle lines between rival news operations are being blurred even more. In 1991 San Francisco's NBC affiliate KRON-TV entered into an agreement with an independent station in the same area to produce a half-hour daily newscast. Under the terms of the agreement KRON would supply all the on-air talent and production staff for the newscast aired on KORY-TV. There are similar deals such as NBC-owned WRC-TV in Washington producing a newscast on rival independent WFTY-TV in Rockville, Maryland; ABC affiliate WNEP-TV producing a newscast in Scranton, Pennsylvania, for Fox Broadcasting Company's affiliate, WOLF-TV; and in Wilkes-Barre, Pennsylvania, Channel 16 providing a half-hour newscast for Channel 38. In effect, news operations are competing with themselves to increase their profitability. Carrying the idea one step further, the News Corporation of American (NCA) will create and run a news department for WPTT-TV in Pittsburgh, apparently the first time an outside contractor will be running a news department for a TV station.

This revolution in TV news did not come about in a vacuum. Developments in the public and private sector shattered the traditional TV news mold. The developments included the relaxed licensing standards of the FCC, the economic squeeze on TV stations and networks, and increased competition from cable. In fact, the remarkable formation of an all-news network, CNN, by Ted Turner changed the way networks operated and perceived their news mission. Before CNN, if you wanted to watch the news on national television you had to wait for the dinnertime half hour of news from one of the three networks. If you missed it, you missed TV network news. But suddenly CNN news was there, not only for a half hour a day, but whenever you wanted it (providing, of course, that you had cable). CNN has indeed become something like a public utility—the telephone, electricity, or water. You turn the faucet on and out pours the news. At the beginning of CNN's operations, the networks hoped that such an operation would be too costly and technologically complex to be achieved by a maverick entrepreneur in Atlanta, Georgia. In fact, in network newsrooms CNN was sometimes derisively known as the Chicken Noodle News. But CNN not only covered the news in a journalistically solid fashion but gained an excellent reputation for being first with major stories and staying on the air with them longer than the networks. CNN became and will remain a force to be reckoned with. Turner proved to the chagrin of the big boys down the block that news could be profitable, not just for thirty minutes a day but around the clock.

Blocked by FCC regulation against owners of entertainment programs, the networks realized that while they couldn't broadcast news around the clock, they could develop news programs that (1) were relatively cheap to produce, (2) could turn a profit, and (3) could do so without necessarily attracting huge audiences. The show "48 Hours" (CBS) can be produced for about $400,000 and returns $800,000–$900,000 in profits per show. This, even though it often finishes low on the list of the nation's most popular shows (at one time sixty-fourth out of eighty-three shows in prime time). Moreover, producers have not been squeamish about wrecking the reputation for seriousness and dignity that network news departments once had, and deserved. Conservative NBC put on a Geraldo Rivera special on devil worship, and ABC and CBS featured re-creations on their news programs. The staid and once-serious network news has begun to look like glitzy local news operations. To the charge that the networks are now money machines and nothing more, and that the old days were better, the answer has come back that CBS once featured Edward R. Murrow visiting the homes of celebrities via television and that Walter Cronkite was once paired with a puppet in an attempt to get ratings for a CBS morning program.

It is not a convincing answer and it is hard to find network executives or journalists who believe it. The networks have always been largely concerned about making money, but at an earlier time they felt keenly their obligation to operate first-class news departments even if it meant running the news departments at a deficit. That sort of thinking is now as obsolete as the coaxial cable.

5

BEHIND THE SCENES:
NUTS AND BOLTS

The number of people required to put together a TV news show is seemingly endless. Their names usually appear about once a week on the crawl at the end of a newscast. The names fly by from the top to the bottom of the screen as an announcer distracts you by asking you to stay tuned for the next program. Nonetheless, if you could transport yourself onto the stage set at the television station you might be surprised at the small number of people actually in the studio. Just a few years ago, most major newscasts had at least three camera operators shooting the in-studio pictures of the anchors, weather people, and other performers on the set. But automation and robotics have changed all that. Now some news programs, including network shows, have robot cameras moving around the studio floor to shoot the various angles selected by the director. If you watch the same newscast night after night, you will notice virtually the same studio shots, in the same order, repeated from show to show. There might be a master wide shot of the anchor sitting handsomely on the set as the announcer introduces the program. This is followed by a medium head-on shot of the anchor as he or she reads the introduction of the first story, followed by videotape. The next story may involved a camera change with the anchor looking left or right, and so on. The camera positions are rehearsed from time to time to present the on-set talent in the best possible light. Since they are predictable, the camera moves are sometimes preprogrammed and stored in computers. When human camera operators are present they can jockey the cameras around as instructed by the director, who is in the control room. The floor manager is in charge of the camera crew on the studio floor. She gets instructions from the control room through a headset system (IFB) and cues the talent by using hand signals. Depending on the program content, the floor manager might alert the anchor to the next "hot camera," counting down the time to the next video or indicating a camera change. The floor manager is the human lifeline between the talent on the set and the control room.

Also out of camera range is the TelePrompTer operator. She is the person who helps the anchor look like he's memorized his script, as he focuses with intensive eye contact on the camera. It is her job to keep the script up to date, make changes, project the final copy onto the TelePrompTer and keep the script scrolling at the reading pace of the anchors. If the TelePrompTer operator scrolls too slowly, the anchors have to slow their reading down; if she scrolls too fast, the anchor could start sounding like Alvin the Chipmunk, trying to keep up the pace. The TelePrompTer operator will use a manual device on which actual pieces of typed script paper are laid out on a moving belt; in more modern facilities, the script may be computerized on a screen. In either event, the script is projected onto a piece of glass located directly over the camera lenses. This allows the anchors to look directly into the camera, as if making eye contact with the viewer, while reading the copy. We've all seen situations where anchors suddenly stop talking and stumble a bit, then look down at their scripts. Chances are something went awry with the TelePrompTer, forcing the anchors to rely on "hard copy," scripts printed on paper used as backups. One of the skills of the better anchors is to cover up these awkward moments, perhaps by ad-libbing. There have been situations where a TelePrompTer has actually died just before airtime, requiring the professionalism of the anchors and crew to prevent a "crash and burn" situation.

Unlike radio, the anchor/readers do not have to be in eye contact with the control room. Electronic "eye contact" is maintained by using electronic monitors. It is not unusual for control rooms to be located in another area, perhaps a different floor or building. There, the producer, director, assistant director (AD), technical director (switcher), audio operator, still store/Chyron operator, video operator, remote coordinator, lighting director, and other editorial personnel monitor and guide the program on the air.

The producer, of course, is the captain of the ship, responsible for getting the broadcast on the air. He makes the key editorial decisions including when a story is aired, its length and position in the program. He works hand in hand with the director who is in charge of the technical phase of the broadcast including calling all the shots, directing cameras, graphics, and remote pickups. The director's rhythm, pace, and shot selection play an important part in the "look" and "feel" of a newscast. The technicians follow the orders of the director who determines what picture goes on the air. When the director calls for a taped story to roll, an engineer in a separate room pushes a button that starts the cassette tape. Each tape has a "countdown" on it—ten, nine, eight, and so on—and with correct timing, the first video picture should come on the air on cue. When that tape has been played, the engineer "cues up" the next tape in a playback machine and again waits for orders from the director.

The assistant director helps the director by cuing, counting down taped segments, and keeping track of the timing of individual stories and the newscast as a whole. She will advise the producer and director if the show is on time or in need of more material. Based on her calculations, material may be cut or added to have the show "time out."

The technical director is the link between the control room and what goes out over the air. The technical director operates a switcher which looks like a control board with a panel of buttons, slides, and switches. The equipment is connected to all the possible sources of news including tape machines, live remotes, the studio, and commercials. Using such devices as Qantels, the switcher has a bag of electronic tricks at her fingertips. She can make a picture appear in a little box, or peel the picture away like a turned page or break it apart on the screen. With the touch of a button, these highly trained technicians can change the picture being transmitted. Of course, with the touch of the wrong button, she could put the wrong picture on the air and wreck a program. It is a tough, high-tension job.

The audio operator is in charge of the sound of the news program. He turns the microphones on and off and feeds the output to the air, "riding" the level to make sure it is not too loud or distorted. A mistake by the audio operator is usually a catastrophe. Imagine, for example, what would happen if someone's microphone were opened at the wrong time. That's what happened to Kathleen Sullivan, a host of "CBS This Morning." While she was on the set for a closed-circuit feed, she did not realize her microphone was open. Her comments, referring to her employer, CBS, as the "Cheap Broadcasting System," went over the air and became a *cause célèbre*.

Besides audio and pictures, written words are still an important element on television news. They help identify people, places, and dates. These titles are usually formed by a computerized device called a character generator. The character generator operates like an electronic typewriter, printing titles on the screen. All the titles used in a newscast are usually prepared beforehand, and stored in a computer for instant retrieval on the air.

The still store/Chyron operator keeps track of the "cgs" and graphics, and electronically produces them on the air, when the director calls for them. Graphics include maps and drawings, often positioned over the shoulder of the anchor. They are supposed to illustrate what the story is about. For example, a story about a murder may be represented by the outline of a body and a gun. These graphics are created by artists who make them with computer imaging. In the early days of television a graphic had to be drawn, then photographed (with the resulting slide projected behind the anchor). Now the graphic is produced, stored, and displayed entirely by computer.

The lighting director's function is to make sure the sets are illuminated properly, especially to show off the anchors to their best advantage. They monitor the scopes and other equipment, and make adjustments as needed.

A relative newcomer to the news control booth is the remote coordinator. She is responsible for arranging for microwave and satellite hook-ups to get on-the-air audio and video from outside the studio. She might arrange for a satellite link thousands of miles away, or a microwave link around the corner. Each must get on the air without a glitch if possible.

While computers have revolutionized most broadcast functions, they have not replaced the makeup artists. They work behind the scenes to make everyone on the air look as good as possible. Using a magic box of tricks and cosmetics the makeup person can take years off the face of an anchor, remove pounds off round faces, and even give a balding anchor the appearance of a man who needs his hair cut.

All of these people operating behind the scenes work to put the newscast on the air. But the meat and potatoes of the newscast is the gathering, preparing, and presentation of the news. Foremost among those responsible for the news is the news director, who hires and fires personnel and who sets the policy and the tone for the news department. We will deal with the news director in detail in the next chapter. Here we need only say that the people who carry out the news director's policy include the assistant news director and the managing editor, who make spot decisions on what events to cover. The producer decides what stories go into a program, which tape is used, the order the stories will be presented in, and the time each will receive. The executive producer is responsible for the overall product.

The assignment editors assign reporters to cover specific stories. Desk assistants, often an entry position, assist the "desk" responsible for covering the news of the day. Production assistants help with the behind-the-scenes nuts and bolts of the broadcast, locating and editing tapes, and putting scripts together. News editors wade through reams of stories from various sources and channel potential items to the producer.

The style of the newscast is often molded by the writing. Writers take facts and transform them into stories, trying to tell them in an interesting, accurate way. Copy from the wire services—facts from reporters and other sources—is the grist for the writer's mill. The craft of the writer is put to the test as each story must conform to the needs of television news. In some cases complex stories must be compressed and told in fifteen or twenty seconds (which means a story will lose all context and nuance). Stories have to be written in the "voice" of the reader, tailor-made for the anchor's style and pace. Introductions to taped pieces and live shots have to set up the material properly and are usually written under great pressure. Videotape editors "cut" the raw tape into broadcast bites, clips, and "B roll" (video for voice-overs). Librarians research facts and dig up needed footage that is filed in a tape room. In addition to these people, there are other technicians, security guards, telephone operators, mail room employees, and others whose efforts contribute to the newscast eventually broadcast.

What you see on television news can be a free-flowing, extemporaneous, live experience at times. But the average prepackaged news story or documentary is anything but that. The "packages" are put together frame by frame, phrase by phrase with hundreds of cuts or edits, stringing together image after image, until a "piece" is completed. A good news package, like any good storytelling, tends to have a beginning, middle, and end with seamless, flowing connections. Accomplishing this requires people who have been trained in the arts and crafts of camera work, writing, editing, narrating, and journalism.

Now that you have some sense of who does what, let's follow an item and see how it gets on a news broadcast. It's four o'clock in the afternoon and eight-year-old Jimmy Barker sees some smoke and fire coming out of a downtown building. He tells his mother, who phones the fire department. Another witness phones the television station and talks to a telephone operator, who connects her to the newsroom. There, a desk assistant takes the call and advises the assignment editor of the details. The assignment editor calls the fire department for additional information. She is told that an office building is on fire at 4567 Broadway. No further information is available.

The assignment editor figures that there could be many people in the building and advises the managing editor, who orders the desk to contact a reporter and crew by two-way radio, sending them to the scene. The managing editor then asks the desk assistant to work the phones, including a cross-reference phone book, which lists phone numbers according to the address. The desk assistant calls a listing for the burning building and someone answers the phone and says he is trapped with six other employees in his sixteenth-floor office. The smoke, he says, is too heavy for them to make their way down the stairs, and the elevators are not running. The desk assistant advises the managing editor of this. The story is shaping up as a major event. A reporter or producer does a recorded interview with the trapped person, and as more confirming information comes in, the managing editor calls the news director. Together they decide that a helicopter should be chartered, and a crew and reporter are dispatched to get the view from the air.

In addition, a "live" truck is ordered to the scene. Its crew will race to the location and find a position where it can send a signal back to the station via microwave. It will raise an antenna and run a cable from the truck to a camera to record pictures of the burning building. The truck, by the way, is self-contained, that is, it makes its own power and has the necessary cameras, recorders, monitors, and microwave transmitting equipment to send pictures back to the television station and if necessary "go live."

The reporter on the scene locates a command post set up by the fire department and there he confirms that there are many people trapped in the building. Fire officials say the blaze seems to be located in the basement. The reporter radios this information back to the newsroom, and begins gathering information from eyewitnesses, taping some of them as the story unfolds. The producer alerts the newsroom personnel that a major story is developing and will probably be the show lead. He is told a chopper is in the air, and there is the possibility of a "live" shot for the show. The wire services are now reporting the fire, and the writers and editors are reading the copy. A report indicates there have been some deaths, and the news director decides to go with the story at the top of the show.

The graphics departments is now told that it should compose a graphic indicating fire in a high-rise. Engineering is advised to stand by for pictures from the live truck and the helicopter. The desk continues to work the phones, getting information that is relayed to the reporters. (Interestingly, the reporters who are in the middle of the action often find themselves isolated from the information flowing into the newsroom from all sources.) The reporters continue to record interviews with survivors and get pictures of people being carried out on stretchers, as fire-fighting equipment and ambulances jam the area. The assignment editor sends a courier to take a field producer to the scene and to return with tape to be edited. The courier returns with the tape, and a writer is assigned to screen and edit it with a technician.

As air time approaches, the reporter at the scene is told he will lead the show and go live with a taped "donut." He will then "throw" to the reporter in the helicopter, who will describe the scene from the air while the airborne camera person transmits pictures back. The engineering department assigns channels for the incoming signals. At airtime, the newscast begins with the anchor telling the audience about the fire, then introducing the reporter on the scene . . . and the broadcast is off and running. The question of why this is news and why it should be the lead on the show are easy to answer. Audiences like to see fires; fires kill, and when people are killed there is drama. And, of course, this is live; it is happening; it creates a sense of urgency and excitement. If it should turn out that the fire was started by an arsonist, the story will take on additional meaning. If it was an "act of God," well, then the story demonstrates the fragility and unpredictability of human life. In any event, it is good television.

News producers and directors may be powerful people but even they cannot make all the news happen live precisely when a newscast is on the air. So most stories that run on the news have to be packaged in advanced. In fact they are even called "packages." Let us take, as an example, an antipollution demonstration that occurs early in the morning. The event will have to be covered on tape. The assignment editor will send a reporter and a crew to the scene. When portable video recording equipment was first used, one person would carry the deck (the recording and playback machine) and another person would operate the video camera. Sometimes a third person would handle the lights and audio. But in these days of miniaturized technology and cost-consciousness, one-person camera crews are frequently used. In any case, the crew arrives on the scene and shoots pictures of the speakers, the crowd, the placard signs, the chanting, a wide shot showing the size of the crowd, close-ups of faces. The camera will shoot from the podium, then from the point of view (POV) of the demonstrators. The raw video, called "B roll," will be varied enough to show the action and give the editor something to work with.

The reporter will direct the camera person to get shots that will tell the story as the reporter sees it. If, for example, the reporter wishes to tell the story from the point of view of one of the protesters who lost her job when a polluting factory was closed down, the protester will be interviewed along with other people who agree and disagree with her. For additional "B roll," the reporter will ask the camera person to pan (smoothly move the camera laterally) from the protesters to the factory that closed down.

With the "B roll" and interviews completed, the reporter will do "stand-ups." The reporter appears on camera introducing and/or linking parts of the story together and/or giving a conclusion to the piece. For dramatic effect the reporter may want to have a picture of the swelling crowd behind him as he does his stand-up close. In that case, he may have to tape his concluding remarks before the story is actually over.

Technically, in the field all material is recorded electromagnetically on cassette tapes. Before editing, the reporter will play the tape and take notes. The final "shot sheet" will indicate the time that each scene takes place. It looks sometimes like this:

:00   Crowd
:15   CU sign
:27   CU faces in crowd
1:46   Mayor Pentle speaks

This "shot sheet" will guide the reporter and editor as they put together a "piece" for the air. This is done by putting together sequence after sequence, then dubbing onto a master tape. The field tape is played back scene by scene on machine one, and recorded on machine two in the desired sequence. The story might start by showing a pan of the protest signs, the crowd, a close-up of a protest sign, the mayor speaking, and faces in the crowd. These shots would be dubbed over, in their new sequence, to a master tape. The natural sound on the tape may be used, including interviews. Where necessary, the reporter will narrate (voice-over") the taped material. When picture and sound are assembled, the story is complete, made up of dozens of edits.

Usually the finished recorded story ("piece") is around two minutes. The reporter may then write a suggested lead to guide the writer who prepares the anchor's introduction to the piece. The reporter must also make a list of the names and titles of the people interviewed for the story, in the order and time they appear on the screen. These, along with dates and locations, will be printed out on the screen to help identify them. A two-minute package may represent a full day's work by a reporter and the labors of a half-dozen technicians. And there will be four to six similar pieces in the average half-hour newscast.

As the elements of the news program are assembled, the producer decides where each of the stories (scripted and taped) will go. Writers have written the scripts, the anchors have read them over, the director and technical staff have the necessary paperwork explaining the order, source, and length of each story, and the show is on the air.

As for the story of the antipollution rally, there will have been little time to explain to the audience what an antipollution rally means. How, for example, did these people get organized? What are the scientific arguments for and against the dangers of pollution in this case? How many other antipollution rallies have been held in this region? Who owns the company that is accused of polluting the environment? What is the position of the local political leaders on this question? And so on. As we have said, television news is in a constant struggle with time, and time is a fierce adversary. Two minutes for the antipollution rally, and that's it. And plenty of pictures. Moreover, as we have tried to suggest in this chapter, the technical demands of television are so complex and unrelenting that everyone concerned is preoccupied with getting matters technically right. Frequently, it is a case of technique triumphing over substance. In TV news, that is the way it goes, most of the time.

6

THE
NEWS DIRECTOR

Earlier, we discussed the question "What is news?" We said that viewers must consider this question seriously with a view toward achieving answers that express their social and political, not to mention spiritual, values. But to most working TV journalists, the answer to the question is moot. For them, the news is determined by what the news director thinks is important, including, of course, his judgment of what stories will draw audiences. In the previous chapter, we mentioned the news director. Here we need to say more about these executives since their decisions do so much to form our consciousness of what the world is like.

Perhaps the first thing to be said about news directors is that they usually don't last long at their jobs. In fact, they tell a story among themselves that aptly describes their burden. It goes like this:

A news director has been fired. He tells the incoming news director that he has left behind three envelopes, each one to be opened after a rating period. The news show does very poorly in the first sweeps period and the new news director goes to the desk and opens the first envelope. It reads "Fire the anchors." When the news director is called to the general manager's office to explain what is wrong with the news department, he answers, "Fire the anchors." The general manager nods in agreement and fires the anchors. The next sweeps period is even worse. Once again the news director is summoned to the general manager's office. Before going in, he remembers the envelopes, and opens the second one. It says "Change the set." When the general manager asks the news director what is wrong with the news department, the news director replies, "We need a new set." The general manager agrees. But the new set doesn't help the ratings either and the next sweeps period is a catastrophe. The news director goes to his desk and opens the last envelope. It reads "Take three envelopes and . . ."

The Radio and Television News Directors Association reports that news directors change jobs an average of every 2.7 years. The reason for the revolving door is the enormous pressure on them to excel not in the journalistic arena but in the ratings.

This does not mean that news directors have no attachment to the traditions of journalism. Most news directors value truth, speed, and accuracy; and they have well-developed ideas about what is "important." But their jobs depend on how many people watch their shows. So they need help. "Help" is a rather ambiguous term. What the general manager or the sales department of a station considers help may not be what the news director considers help. For example, take the case of news consultants.

Consultants are hired by stations to find ways to increase the ratings of news shows, and to do so quickly. The usual way to proceed is by emphasizing "hair-spray ethics" at the expense of solid journalism. Consultants, therefore, may not be interested in or knowledgeable about journalism. They can say if an "on-air talent" is likable and a "good communicator" but are usually unqualified to judge the quality of news reports. The methods of consultants differ from company to company and from station to station. But basically they look at the news programs and recommend ways of attracting more viewers—that is to say, customers—to it. It's that simple.

For example, using techniques of market research, a consultant may draw a profile of the average viewer the station wants to attract. The profile is a statistical compilation of, among other things, the age, economic status, and consumer habits of the audience. The consultant then carefully observes the anchors and reporters to determine if they fit the viewer profile. Do these viewers like to watch these anchors and reporters? To assist in answering this question, a consultant may form a "focus group" to get the reaction of "average" viewers to the present anchors and reporters, as well as to their potential replacements. A focus group is nothing more than a collection of representative viewers who watch tapes of programs under controlled conditions, and report their reactions. Consultants rely heavily on focus groups because it is difficult to guess what audiences will like or hate. It is best to ask "average" viewers and extrapolate from there. The issue can be quite complicated. Male viewers, for example, may not like a certain woman anchor, believing her to be too aggressive. Women viewers may find a female anchor too seductive. Men may like a certain male anchor because of his authority; women may dislike the same anchor for the same reason. To feed the focus groups, major consulting firms such as Frank Magid Associates in Marion, Iowa, have huge computerized files with videos of almost every on-air reporter in the country. If a consultant recommends a blond, blue-eyed, twenty-seven-year-old female reporter with five years' experience, chances are there's one in the file.

In addition to focus groups, consultants frequently depend on "track records," that is, how an anchor or reporter has performed in the ratings in the past. The theory is that if an anchor has done well in one market, he or she will "travel" well and get good ratings in another market. The theory does not always fit the facts. There are many cases of anchors who have been unable to duplicate their ratings' success from one market to another. But obviously some anchors can bring their popularity with them, and indeed that is their main talent.

What all of this means is that consultants may be able to help a news director keep his or her job. Or may not. But it is clear that consultants usually are not competent to help the news director in deciding what is worth reporting. For this, most news directors rely on fairly traditional sources.

For example, many story ideas originate in newspapers, which traditionally have larger staffs and more "beat" reporters than TV stations. The headline stories of newspapers are developed and reported on the evening news by general-assignment reporters. Other story ideas come from the police and fire department radio reports of crimes, fires, and accidents. Viewers sometimes phone in news tips. And, of course, staff members may develop stories based on their own observations. For example, a reporter might notice that a department store isn't too crowded during a normally busy season. That might be an indication that the local economy is on a downswing. There could be a story in that. Or a reporter, noticing that there are extra men in the mayor's security force, may uncover the news that a threat has been made on the mayor's life. Many stories are originated by press secretaries issuing press releases ("handouts") to the news media. With the speed and reduced cost of sending material to networks and individual stations via satellite, video press releases have taken on a new significance. The Radio and Television News Directors Association recommends that news programs label material supplied by non-news sources, but often this advice is ignored. *TV Guide* in its February 22, 1992, issue documented story after story in which video supplied by lobbying groups, product manufacturers, and political candidates was used in news programs without labeling the source. The examples included a segment on the hazards of automatic safety belts in cars, a "story" run on the "CBS Evening News" on June 13, 1991. The tape showed a car being tipped on its side, the door opening, and the strap allowing a dummy to fall out and be crushed beneath the car. The casual viewer would assume the tape was shot by CBS News. But in fact it was prepared by the Institute for Injury Reduction, a lobbying group largely supported by lawyers whose clients often sue auto companies for crash-related injuries. According to Neilsen Media Research, roughly 80 percent of the country's news directors say they use video news release (VNR) material at least several times a month. According to Medialink, a major distributor of video releases, four hundred VNRs were made available to news departments in 1991. With the relatively low cost of about $20,000 per release and satellite transponder time costing $600 an hour for distribution, many video releases will shower down from the heavens to more picture-hungry television news operations in the years to come.

Of course, all kinds of press releases increase enormously during political campaigns, and are supplemented by what is called a "photo opportunity." In this situation, the print press and TV press are invited to "see all but speak not" to the candidate posing under the lights. Reporters usually ask questions anyway, and, typically, officials who do not wish to answer pretend they don't know what has been asked. "Sorry, Sam, I can't hear you."

The "photo op" is, obviously, a particularly important source of news for television. In America, politicians are largely known by their image on television. As a consequence, politicians like to do things that show them in a positive light—visiting a hospital, welcoming a visitor from another country, observing the aftermath of a train wreck, and so on. News directors accommodate the visual needs of politicians because television needs pictures. There is not much television news to be made of a congressman's twenty-two-page position paper on the decline of education in a city. But a photo op of the congressman inspecting a decaying building is useful.

A considerable number of events are staged to attract television cameras. When a political candidate goes to a closed factory or stands outside the slums so that a camera can capture the scene, the candidate is manipulating television coverage. Some people get so good at figuring out how to do this that they get paid for it. Of course, they are not called manipulators. They are called political consultants.

Roger Ailes, who ran the Bush media campaign in 1988, claims that three things always get covered by television: visuals, attacks, and mistakes. Despite the networks spending about $30 million each to cover presidential political campaigns, NBC's chief congressional correspondent Andrea Mitchell thinks political strategists and consultants are learning to manipulate television too effectively, staging events and orchestrating sound bites and photo ops to promote their candidates. She quotes Larry Speakes, Ronald Reagan's press secretary, as saying to the news media, "Don't tell us how to stage the news, and we won't tell you how to cover it." Mitchell believes that managed television news coverage has made it difficult for reporters to provide the necessary scutiny of Presidents in office or presidential candidates because deadlines, competition, and limited access make meaningful coverage close to impossible. Mitchell asks, "Aside from pictures, what do we remember from the last campaign? We remember the battle of sound bites, those snappy one-liners like 'Read my lips, no new taxes.'" She laments that "the average sound bite has shrunk, from forty-five seconds ten years ago, to fifteen seconds in 1985, to nine seconds in the '88 campaign. It makes you wonder just what a candidate can tell a voter in nine seconds."

Former CBS legal correspondent Fred Graham reports that back in 1975 when Richard Salant and Walter Cronkite dominated CBS News, the average sound bite ran sixteen seconds. Ten years later, when Van Gordon Sauter and Dan Rather were the dominating forces, the average length of a sound bite in one of Graham's pieces was nine seconds. Graham complains that some sound bites that survived the editing process were so short as to defy understanding. Two independent studies since the 1968 election confirm the trend. Kiku Adatto, a Harvard University sociologist, and Daniel Hallin, a University of California at San Diego political scientist, both showed in their work that sound bites of presidential candidates on the network evening news had shrunk by more than seventy-five percent between 1968 and 1988. Dr. Hallin argues that one gains a broader understanding of a candidate's character and the logic of his or her argument in a paragraph than in a ten-second sound bite.

News directors are of course aware of all this; indeed, most of them probably disapprove of photo ops, sound bites, and staged events. But they are in a competitive business, under pressure from executive producers, sales managers, and sponsors to draw audiences. And they can never forget that lurking in their desks is the envelope that prophecies their end. And so news directors will not disregard staged events, not even those that appear in the daybook.

The daybook is in fact a major source of television stories. Daybook items are listings of planned daily events. They include the time and place of scheduled activities, including official functions such as press conferences and ceremonies at City Hall, press agents' creations (e.g., Lucille Ball look-alike contests), and events that are supposed to be spontaneous but often are not— for example, protests and demonstrations. In setting up the daily news "budget" the news director and the man-

aging editor often make assignments from the daybook.
And a good news director understands that on a slow
August Sunday a photo opportunity of Miss Coney Island
sitting on a block of cold ice might make an item on the
eleven o'clock news.

From what we have said so far, you will conclude
correctly that the task of the news director is extremely
complex. Multiple decisions must be made, taking into
account not only the question "What is news?" but, more
important, "What is television news?" And while on any
given day most of the audience accepts without complaint
the wisdom of the news director's decisions, there are
groups of people who monitor these decisions, almost
daily, to determine if they are being fairly treated; or if
the news director's decisions have violated some political
or social ideal. They are called "watchdog groups," and
from the point of view of a news director, they are little
else but an unwanted complication.

These groups have a wide range of interests, from
Democrats who believe they're getting less airtime than
Republicans to fundamentalists checking for obscenities
on programs. They are not reluctant to make their views
known, and to try to bring pressure on programmers to
change the content of shows. For example, a liberal
watchdog group called FAIR (Fairness and Accuracy in
Reporting) has criticized the "MacNeil/Lehrer News-
Hour" and "Nightline," claiming that these programs
have a white male, conservative leaning. FAIR tracked
the "MacNeil/Lehrer NewsHour" and "Nightline" from

February 6 through August 14, 1989, analyzing the guest lists. FAIR concluded that both shows presented narrow political viewpoints, with the "MacNeil/Lehrer News-Hour" full of guests from "the Washington-Wall Street corridors, with very little output from anyone else." Overall, FAIR found that 90 percent of "MacNeil/Lehrer's" guests were white, 82 percent male; that nineteen frequent guests on "MacNeil/Lehrer" (with three or more appearances) included nine U.S. officials, six of whom were conservatives; that only one of the seventeen guests on environmental issues was a representative of an environmental group; and that 89 percent of "Nightline" guests were white and 82 percent male.

Naturally, the shows defended themselves. "MacNeil/Lehrer" executive producer Les Crystal pointed out that FAIR failed to take into account the lengthy tape reports that are a significant part of the program. As to the predominance of white males, well (the defense goes), most officials in American politics *are* white males. If FAIR had studied the interviews of and reports about professional basketball players, it would have found 70 percent or more featured black males. So goes the defense. But putting news directors on the defensive is by no means a bad thing. Watchdog groups serve as a feedback mechanism, forcing producers and news directors to defend their decisions, and, sometimes, to alter their habitual ways of thinking. On the other hand, sensitivity to feedback can produce cowardly responses.

Networks with an eye on sponsors' satisfaction and stockholders' dividends are particularly fearful about charges of racial or sexual bias. In February of 1990, Andy Rooney was suspended by CBS, accused of making a racist remark in a magazine interview. A public uproar ensued. The fact that Rooney denied the charge and had been an honored employee with forty years' experience did not prevent the network from suspending him from the popular program "60 Minutes." The ratings of the program dropped and the network, apparently fearing the economic consequences, reinstated Rooney.

But the incident demonstrates two important points. First, TV executives are hypersensitive to public criticism. Second, a principal consideration in responding to public criticism is profit and loss. The news director who can arrange matters so that public criticism is kept to a minimum, and profits remain high, does not have to open the last envelope in the desk drawer.

7

REENACTMENTS
AND DOCUDRAMAS,
OR NO NEWS
IS STILL NEWS

On several occasions, former President Ronald Reagan enjoyed telling how he re-created Chicago Cubs' games in his years as a baseball announcer. In the early days of radio, details of baseball games were telegraphed down the line to radio stations where announcers would re-create the game without seeing it. When the information was slow in coming, the announcers were forced to use their imaginations to fill in the details. They would, for example, describe how the pitcher was taking his time, was picking up the resin bag and checking the new ball thrown to him by the umpire. In other words, the announcer would kill time until the telegraph details started flowing again. What the announcer said might not have been the truth but it was good theater. To make even better theater, the announcer would hit a stick against a piece of wood to simulate the sound of a bat hitting a ball. It sounded real but it wasn't. It was a baseball game as imagined by the announcer, a re-creation—we might even say, a docudrama.

Re-creations were used from time to time on radio programs other than baseball games. For example, the program "The March of Time" was a form of docudrama employing actors who impersonated historic figures such as Hitler, Churchill, and Roosevelt. The tradition carried over to television. "You Are There" aired from 1953 to 1957 and again in 1971 for one season. Its host was Walter Cronkite. The program re-created various historical events complete with conversations no one had ever heard. To his credit, Cronkite is on record as believing that historical re-creations have "no place in a news division," that, in effect, they are devices to be used to entertain, and not for anything else.

But that was long ago, before the line separating news and entertainment became blurred, before news programming became a "cash cow." Television's need to fill the blank screen brought re-creations back in ways that might even surprise Ronald Reagan. Instead of an anchor simply talking about an event on camera, reenactments allow actors and other masters of stagecraft to formulate a scene that approximated events from the past. Instead of a blank screen we have a simulation of reality, a reenactment.

Generally speaking, television executives don't see reenactments as a problem, primarily because reenactments make engrossing television. But some critics claim that re-creations mislead the viewer into thinking he or she is watching a recording of the real thing. Perhaps the most famous example of a re-creation gone astray took place in July 1989. ABC's "World News Tonight" showed footage of U.S. diplomat Felix Bloch handing a briefcase to a Soviet agent. The scene was not labeled as a re-creation. The word "simulation" or some other warning, such as "what you are seeing, we made up," was accidentally left off the screen, leaving viewers with the impression they were watching the actual taped event. The entire scene was broadcast for only ten seconds but its impact was great. It focused attention on the problem inherent in "re-creating" reality.

These problems do not disappear even when a re-creation is properly labeled. For example, the CBS news series "Saturday Night with Connie Chung" presented the story of Abbie Hoffman's last days. Hoffman, after a colorful career as an activist for various causes, committed suicide. The program purported to reveal the last moments of Hoffman's life. His last words, reenacted, were as follows:

ABBIE: I'm okay, Jack. I'm okay. Yeah, I'm out of bed. I got my feet on the floor. Yeah. Two feet. I'll see you Wednesday? Thursday. I'll always be with you, Jack. Don't worry.

Viewers knew, of course, that Hoffman was already dead so that they could not be hearing his last words as he spoke them. But many believed, and had a right to believe, that someone had recorded the event and that these were Hoffman's actual words. They weren't. They were words pieced together by interviews and then scripted by a writer. Does it matter that the words attributed to Abbie Hoffman in his last moments were never uttered?

Some say it doesn't. In fact, besides using re-creations for short segments on news shows, TV producers have created whole programs of simulated reality. They are called docudramas. These usually use real news stories for the starting point of a story line, then weave in events created by a writer. These events may or may not be true, but producers defend docudramas by arguing that the audience understands that it is not watching the actual event. The fact that studies show that audiences tend to absorb information from television even though they forget where that information originated does not trouble producers of docudramas.

Producers like docudramas for a variety of reasons. For one thing, they take the form of a theatrical event with a beginning, middle, and end, with "time outs" for commercials. Actual news events, of course, are not always so tidy. In real-life dramas, heroes get killed, hostages are sometimes not released, and the villain is not always brought to justice. Most newsworthy events are not concluded in neat thirty- or sixty-minute segments. A docudrama can remedy unhappy or unjust conclusions by packaging them in palatable forms.

Another reason some producers like docudramas is their low cost. A re-created one-hour docudrama might cost $400,000–$500,000, or roughly half of what a similar theatrical drama would cost using popular actors, good writers, scenic designers, and directors.

The lines between re-creations and reality are so muddled that some news programs have even used Hollywood films to illustrate news stories. There is nothing producers or news directors fear more than a void, a black hole in a newscast, as for example, when the anchor is talking about a subject and there is no newsreel footage to go with the comments. What to do? One answer is simply to use excerpts from Hollywood films. On one CBS network newscast, while Dan Rather reported on a new exploration of the *Titanic* wreckage, the picture on the screen was of a movie depicting the sinking of the *Titanic*, complete with wet actors manning the lifeboats. It was enough to give serious journalists a sinking feeling. On "NBC News with Tom Brokaw," a reporter used footage from the movie *The Spy Who Came in from the Cold* to illustrate the changing roles of the CIA now that the Soviet Union's menace seems to be fading. The next logical step would be to run a clip of a John Wayne movie showing battle footage when discussing the fighting during World War II, or any war that happened to be around. To our knowledge, that hasn't happened . . . yet.

So where should the lines be drawn? Is it acceptable for applause to be dubbed in on footage of a concert, or sirens in a police-car chase scene, or gunfire in battle footage? Is it ethical for a television journalist to use a "reverse question," that is, the technique of taking pictures of a reporter asking the questions he used during an earlier interview, then splicing the questions into a finished tape? We know what answers Edward R. Murrow would give to most of these questions. He once addressed them, and made the following unambiguous remark: "There will always be some errors in news gathering, but the tricks that microphones, cameras, and film make possible must never be contrived to pass off as news events that were fabricated to document an event that we missed or which may never have happened."

Murrow is generally regarded as the man who established the standards of TV news, and we can assume his microphone would short out were he to know about the uses made of re-creations today. Indeed, we can imagine he would have some harsh words for "pseudo-news" shows such as Phil Donahue's and Geraldo Rivera's. These programs are not under the control of news departments but draw part of their appeal from the fact that they involve real people and real events. They are television's version of "yellow journalism," typically dealing with sensational, weird, or perverse stories.

During one ratings period in 1989, the "Geraldo"

show featured the following subjects: "Prison Mother-hood," "Lady Lifers: Bad Girls Behind Bars," "Teen Prostitutes," "Women Who Date Married Men," "Girls Who Can't Say 'No!,' " "Murderers Who Should Never Get Out of Prison," "Campus Rape," "Illicit, Illegal, Im-moral: Selling of Forbidden Desires," "Parents of Slain Prostitutes," "Cocaine Cowgirls," "Chippendales," "Battered Lesbians," "Contract to Kill: Running from the Mafia," "Men Who Marry Prostitutes," "Transsexual Transformations," "Angels of Death," and "Secret Lives of Stars"—all this within one three-week period.

The defense for this kind of programing proceeds along the following lines. First, such programming draws huge audiences, which suggests that people are interested in both the subject matter and the subjects. Second, the high profitability of the shows allows the hosts to include programs devoted to more acceptable news content—for example, an interview with the Secretary of Defense or a discussion of industrial pollution. The audience is at-tracted by the promise of the bizarre, then is exposed to serious issues. Third, programs about battered lesbians, girls who can't say "no," and parents of slain prostitutes *are* news, and serious news, at that. They tell as much or more about the state of our society than do 90 percent of the stories on any daily network news show. They are a form of documentary journalism; they reveal to us the pain, humiliation, and confusion of real people trying to cope with an intractable reality.

The answer to these arguments is that such programming is nothing more than a highly profitable freak show, exploiting the insatiable curiosity of audiences for what is strange and forbidden. The audience members are voyeurs, peeking, as it were, into the bedrooms or living rooms of people who are desperately seeking a momentary sense of celebrity. Besides, all of this serves as a diversion from the urgent issues of the day. What people don't know can kill them (to borrow from Fred Friendly, formerly of CBS News). To this might be added that what people do know can keep them from knowing what they must know. In other words, the "pseudo-news" show fixes people's attention on what is peripheral to an understanding of their lives, and may even disable them from distinguishing what is relevant from what is not.

In fact, a somewhat similar set of arguments is made against the docudramas and re-creations (especially those done within the context of news shows). It proceeds as follows: A re-creation can be as engrossing as a program about men who marry prostitutes. But as the latter diverts attention from what is necessary to know, the former severs the trust that citizens must have in their sources of information. For example, consider the following lead sentence from a story in *The New York Times*, August 5, 1991: "More than 500 passengers and crew members were saved yesterday in a tense rescue operation when the Greek cruise liner *Oceanos* . . . foundered and sank in high winds and heavy seas two miles off the South African coast."

Now, let's pretend that you learned that the *Times* story was in error;—that only 324 passengers were saved (500 makes the rescue operation appear more effective); that there were no high winds and heavy seas (that was included to make the event more dramatic); and that the boat did not sink after the passengers were removed but made it safely back to port (a sinking boat makes a better story than a merely damaged boat). You would, we imagine, abandon whatever trust you have in *The New York Times* as a reliable source of news. We imagine further that you would not be impressed with an explanation claiming that the alterations were made to give the story more drama. Moreover, if you think our example exaggerates the extent to which a TV docudrama may depart from reality, we should observe that in the mini-series depicting the life of Peter the Great, there was a scene in which Peter meets with Isaac Newton, a meeting which never took place except in the imaginations of the writer, director, and producer of the program. The two of them did live, roughly, at the same time; Peter died in 1725, Newton in 1727. Is this a justification for a scene in which they have a conversation? Perhaps—if you take the view that *all* television is only a form of entertainment. Not at all—if you take a more rigorous position, that when entertainment conflicts with truth, truth must prevail.

8

THE BIAS OF LANGUAGE, THE BIAS OF PICTURES

When a television news show distorts the truth by altering or manufacturing facts (through re-creations), a television viewer is defenseless even if a re-creation is properly labeled. Viewers are still vulnerable to misinformation since they will not know (at least in the case of docudramas) what parts are fiction and what parts are not. But the problems of verisimilitude posed by re-creations pale to insignificance when compared to the problems viewers face when encountering a straight (no-monkey-business) show. All news shows, in a sense, are re-creations in that what we hear and see on them are attempts to represent actual events, and are not the events themselves. Perhaps, to avoid ambiguity, we might call all news shows "re-presentations" instead of "re-creations." These re-presentations come to us in two forms: language and pictures. The question then arises: what do viewers have to know about language and pictures in order to be properly armed to defend themselves against the seductions of eloquence (to use Bertrand Russell's apt phrase)?

Let us take language first. Below are three principles that, in our opinion, are an essential part of the analytical equipment a viewer must bring to any encounter with a news show.

1.
Whatever anyone says something is, it isn't.

This sounds more complex—and maybe more pretentious—than it actually is. What it means is that there is a difference between the world of events and the world of words about events. The job of an honest reporter is to try to find words and the appropriate tone in presenting them that will come as close to evoking the event as possible. But since no two people will use exactly the same words to describe an event, we must acknowledge that for every verbal description of an event, there are multiple possible alternatives. You may demonstrate this to your own satisfaction by writing a two-paragraph description of a dinner you had with at least two other people, then asking the others who were present if each of them would also write, independently, a two-paragraph description of the "same" dinner. We should be very surprised if all of the descriptions include the same words, in the same order, emphasize the same things, and express the same feelings. In other words, "the dinner itself" is largely a nonverbal event. The words people use to describe this event are not the event itself and are only abstracted re-presentations of the event. What does this mean for a television viewer? It means that the viewer must never assume that the words spoken on a television news show are exactly what happened. Since there are so many alternative ways of describing what happened, the viewer must be on guard against assuming that he or she has heard "the absolute truth."

2.

Language operates at various levels of abstraction.

This means that there is a level of language whose purpose is to *describe* an event. There is also a level of language whose purpose is to *evaluate* an event. Even more, there is a level of language whose purpose is to *infer* what is unknown on the basis of what is known. The usual way to make these distinctions clear is through sentences such as the following three:

Manny Freebus is 5'8" and weighs 235 pounds.

Manny Freebus is grossly fat.

Manny Freebus eats too much.

The first sentence may be said to be language as pure description. It involves no judgments and no inferences. The second sentence is a description of sorts, but is mainly a judgment that the speaker makes of the "event" known as Manny Freebus. The third sentence is an inference based on observations the speaker has made. It is, in fact, a statement about the unknown based on the known. As it happens, we know Manny Freebus and can tell you that he eats no more than the average person but suffers from a glandular condition which keeps him overweight. Therefore, anyone who concluded from observing Manny's shape that he eats too much has made a false inference. A good guess, but false nonetheless.

You can watch television news programs from now until doomsday and never come across any statement about Manny Freebus. But you will constantly come across the three kinds of statements we have been discussing—descriptions, judgments, and inferences. And it is important for a viewer to distinguish among them. For example, you might hear an anchor introduce a story by saying: "Today Congress ordered an investigation of the explosive issue of whether Ronald Reagan's presidential campaign made a deal with Iran in 1980 to delay the release of American hostages until after the election." This statement is, of course, largely descriptive, but includes the judgmental word "explosive" as part of the report. We need hardly point out that what is explosive to one person may seem trivial to another. We do not say that the news writer has no business to include his or her judgment of this investigation. We do say that the viewer has to be aware that a judgment has been made. In fact, even the phrase "made a deal" (why not "arranged with Iran"?) has a somewhat sleazy connotation that implies a judgment of sorts. If, in the same news report, we are told that the evidence for such a secret deal is weak and that only an investigation with subpoena power can establish the truth, we must know that we have left the arena of factual language and have moved into the land of inference. An investigation with subpoena power may be a good idea but whether or not it can establish the truth is a guess on the journalist's part, and a viewer ought to know that.

3.

Almost all words have connotative meanings.

This suggests that even when attempting to use purely descriptive language, a journalist cannot avoid expressing an attitude about what he or she is saying. For example, here is the opening sentence of an anchor's report about national examinations: "For the first time in the nation's history, high-level education policymakers have designed the elements for a national examination system similar to the one advocated by President Bush." This sentence certainly looks like it is pure description although it is filled with ambiguities. Is this the first time in our history that this has been done? Or only the first time that high-level education policymakers have done it? Or is it the first time something has been designed that is similar to what the President has advocated? But let us put those questions aside. (After all, there are limits to how analytical one ought to be.) Instead, we might concentrate on such words as "high-level," "policymakers," and "designed." Speaking for ourselves, we are by no means sure that we know what a "high-level policymaker" is, although it sounds awfully impressive. It is certainly better than a "low-level policymaker," although how one would distinguish between the two is a bit of a mystery. Come to think of it, a low-level "policymaker" must be pretty good, too, since anyone who makes policy must be important. It comes as no surprise, therefore, that what was done was "designed." To design something usually implies careful thought, preparation, organization, and coherence. People design buildings, bridges, and furniture. If your experience has been anything like ours, you will know that reports are almost never designed; they are usually "thrown together," and it is quite a compliment to say that a report was designed. The journalist who paid this compliment was certainly entitled to do it even though he may not have been aware of what he was doing. He probably thought he had made a simple description, avoiding any words that would imply favor or disfavor. But if so, he was defeated in his effort because language tends to be emotion-laden. Because it is people who do the talking, the talk almost always includes a feeling, an attitude, a judgment. In a sense, every language contains the history of a people's feelings about the world. Our words are baskets of emotion. Smart journalists, of course, know this. And so do smart audiences. Smart audiences don't blame anyone for this state of affairs. They are, however, prepared for it.

It is not our intention to provide here a mini-course in semantics. Even if we could, we are well aware that no viewer could apply analytic principles all the time or even much of the time. Anchors and reporters talk too fast and too continuously for any of us to monitor most of their sentences. Besides, who would want to do that for most of the stories on a news show? If you have a sense of what is important, you will probably judge most news stories to be fluff, or nonsense, or irrelevancies, not worthy of your analytic weaponry. But there are times when stories appear that are of major significance from your point of view. These are the times when your level of attention will reach a peak and you must call upon your best powers of interpretation. In those moments, you need to draw on whatever you know about the relationship between language and reality; about the distinctions among statements of fact, judgment, and inference; about the connotative meanings of words. When this is done properly, viewers are no longer passive consumers of news but active participants in a kind of dialogue between a news show and themselves. A viewer may even find that he or she is "talking back to the television set" (which is the title of a book by former FCC commissioner Nicholas Johnson). In our view, nothing could be healthier for the sanity and well-being of our nation than to have ninety million viewers talking back to their television news shows every night and twice on Sunday.

Now we must turn to the problem of pictures. It is often said that a picture is worth a thousand words. Maybe so. But it is probably equally true that one word is worth a thousand pictures, at least sometimes—for example, when it comes to understanding the world we live in. Indeed, the whole problem with news on television comes down to this: all the words uttered in an hour of news coverage could be printed on one page of a newspaper. And the world cannot be understood in one page. Of course, there is a compensation: television offers pictures, and the pictures move. Moving pictures are a kind of language in themselves, but the language of pictures differs radically from oral and written language, and the differences are crucial for understanding television news.

To begin with, pictures, especially single pictures, speak only in particularities. Their vocabulary is limited to concrete representation. Unlike words and sentences, a picture does not present to us an idea or concept about the world, except as we use language itself to convert the image to idea. By itself, a picture cannot deal with the unseen, the remote, the internal, the abstract. It does not speak of "man," only of *a* man; not of "tree," only of *a* tree. You cannot produce an image of "nature," any more than an image of "the sea." You can only show a particular fragment of the here-and-now—a cliff of a certain terrain, in a certain condition of light; a wave at a moment in time, from a particular point of view. And just as "nature" and "the sea" cannot be photographed, such larger abstractions as truth, honor, love, and falsehood cannot be talked about in the lexicon of individual pictures. For "showing of" and "talking about" are two very different kinds of processes: individual pictures give us the world as object; language, the world as idea. There is no such thing in nature as "man" or "tree." The universe offers no such categories or simplifications; only flux and infinite variety. The picture documents and celebrates the particularities of the universe's infinite variety. Language makes them comprehensible.

Of course, moving pictures, video with sound, may bridge the gap by juxtaposing images, symbols, sound, and music. Such images can present emotions and rudimentary ideas. They can suggest the panorama of nature and the joys and miseries of humankind.

Picture—smoke pouring from the window, cut to people coughing, an ambulance racing to a hospital, a tombstone in a cemetery.

Picture—jet planes firing rockets, explosions, lines of

foreign soldiers surrendering, the American flag waving in the wind.

Nonetheless, keep in mind that when terrorists want to prove to the world that their kidnap victims are still alive, they photograph them holding a copy of a recent newspaper. The dateline on the newspaper provides the proof that the photograph was taken on or after that date. Without the help of the written word, film and videotape cannot portray temporal dimensions with any precision. Consider a film clip showing an aircraft carrier at sea. One might be able to identify the ship as Soviet or American, but there would be no way of telling where in the world the carrier was, where it was headed, or when the pictures were taken. It is only through language—words spoken over the pictures or reproduced in them—that the image of the aircraft carrier takes on specific meaning.

Still, it is possible to enjoy the image of the carrier for its own sake. One might find the hugeness of the vessel interesting; it signifies military power on the move. There is a certain drama in watching the planes come in at high speeds and skid to a stop on the deck. Suppose the ship were burning: that would be even more interesting. This leads to an important point about the language of pictures. Moving pictures favor images that change. That is why violence and dynamic destruction find their way onto television so often. When something is destroyed violently it is altered in a highly visible way; hence the entrancing power of fire. Fire gives visual form to the ideas of consumption, disappearance, death—the thing that burned is actually taken away by fire. It is at this very basic level that fires make a good subject for television news. Something was here, now it's gone, and the change is recorded on film.

Earthquakes and typhoons have the same power. Before the viewer's eyes the world is taken apart. If a television viewer has relatives in Mexico City and an earthquake occurs there, then he or she may take a special interest in the images of destruction as a report from a specific place and time; that is, one may look at television pictures for information about an important event. But film of an earthquake can be interesting even if the viewer cares nothing about the event itself. Which is only to say, as we noted earlier, that there is another way of participating in the news—as a spectator who desires to be entertained. Actually to see buildings topple is exciting, no matter where the buildings are. The world turns to dust before our eyes.

Those who produce television news in America know that their medium favors images that move. That is why they are wary of "talking heads," people who simply appear in front of a camera and speak. When talking heads appear on television, there is nothing to record or document, no change in process. In the cinema the situation is somewhat different. On a movie screen, close-ups of a good actor speaking dramatically can sometimes be interesting to watch. When Clint Eastwood narrows his eyes and challenges his rival to shoot first, the spectator sees the cool rage of the Eastwood character take visual form, and the narrowing of the eyes is dramatic. But much of the effect of this small movement depends on the size of the movie screen and the darkness of the theater, which make Eastwood and his every action "larger than life."

The television screen is smaller than life. It occupies about 15 percent of the viewer's visual field (compared to about 70 percent for the movie screen). It is not set in a darkened theater closed off from the world but in the viewer's ordinary living space. This means that visual changes must be more extreme and more dramatic to be interesting on television. A narrowing of the eyes will not do. A car crash, an earthquake, a burning factory are much better.

With these principles in mind, let us examine more closely the structure of a typical newscast, and here we will include in the discussion not only the pictures but all the nonlinguistic symbols that make up a television news show. For example, in America, almost all news shows begin with music, the tone of which suggests important events about to unfold. The music is very important, for it equates the news with various forms of drama and ritual—the opera, for example, or a wedding procession—in which musical themes underscore the meaning of the event. Music takes us immediately into the realm of the symbolic, a world that is not to be taken literally. After all, when events unfold in the real world, they do so without musical accompaniment. More symbolism follows. The sound of teletype machines can be heard in the studio, not because it is impossible to screen this noise out, but because the sound is a kind of music in itself. It tells us that data are pouring in from all corners of the globe, a sensation reinforced by the world map in the background (or clocks noting the time on different continents). The fact is that teletype machines are rarely used in TV news rooms, having been replaced by silent computer terminals. When seen, they have only a symbolic function.

Already, then, before a single news item is introduced, a great deal has been communicated. We know that we are in the presence of a symbolic event, a form of theater in which the day's events are to be dramatized. This theater takes the entire globe as its subject, although it may look at the world from the perspective of a single nation. A certain tension is present, like the atmosphere in a theater just before the curtain goes up. The tension is represented by the music, the staccato beat of the teletype machines, and often the sight of news workers scurrying around typing reports and answering phones. As a technical matter, it would be no problem to build a set in which the newsroom staff remained off camera, invisible to the viewer, but an important theatrical effect would be lost. By being busy on camera, the workers help communicate urgency about the events at hand, which suggests that situations are changing so rapidly that constant revision of the news is necessary.

The staff in the background also helps signal the

importance of the person in the center, the anchor, "in command" of both the staff and the news. The anchor plays the role of host. He or she welcomes us to the newscast and welcomes us back from the different locations we visit during the filmed reports.

Many features of the newscast help the anchor to establish the impression of control. These are usually equated with production values in broadcasting. They include such things as graphics that tell the viewer what is being shown, or maps and charts that suddenly appear on the screen and disappear on cue, or the orderly progression from story to story. They also include the absence of gaps, or "dead time," during the broadcast, even the simple fact that the news starts and ends at a certain hour. These common features are thought of as purely technical matters, which a professional crew handles as a matter of course. But they are also symbols of a dominant theme of television news: the imposition of an orderly world—called "the news"—upon the disorderly flow of events.

While the form of a news broadcast emphasizes tidiness and control, its content can best be described as fragmented. Because time is so precious on television, because the nature of the medium favors dynamic visual images, and because the pressures of a commercial structure require the news to hold its audience above all else, there is rarely any attempt to explain issues in depth or place events in their proper context. The news moves nervously from a warehouse fire to a court decision, from a guerrilla war to a World Cup match, the quality of the film most often determining the length of the story. Certain stories show up only because they offer dramatic pictures. Bleachers collapse in South America: hundreds of people are crushed—a perfect television news story, for the cameras can record the face of disaster in all its anguish. Back in Washington, a new budget is approved by Congress. Here there is nothing to photograph because a budget is not a physical event; it is a document full of language and numbers. So the producers of the news will show a photo of the document itself, focusing on the cover where it says "Budget of the United States of America." Or sometimes they will send a camera crew to the government printing plant where copies of the budget are produced. That evening, while the contents of the budget are summarized by a voice-over, the viewer sees stacks of documents being loaded into boxes at the government printing plant. Then a few of the budget's more important provisions will be flashed on the screen in written form, but this is such a time-consuming process—using television as a printed page—that the producers keep it to a minimum. In short, the budget is not televisable, and for that reason its time on the news must be brief. The bleacher collapse will get more time that evening.

While appearing somewhat chaotic, these disparate stories are not just dropped in the news program helter-skelter. The appearance of a scattershot story order is really orchestrated to draw the audience from one story to the next—from one section to the next—through the commercial breaks to the end of the show. The story order is constructed to hold and build the viewership rather than place events in context or explain issues in depth.

Of course, it is a tendency of journalism in general to concentrate on the surface of events rather than underlying conditions; this is as true for the newspaper as it is for the newscast. But several features of television undermine whatever efforts journalists may make to give sense to the world. One is that a television broadcast is a series of events that occur in sequence, and the sequence is the same for all viewers. This is not true for a newspaper page, which displays many items simultaneously, allowing readers to choose the order in which they read them. If newspaper readers want only a summary of the latest tax bill, they can read the headline and the first paragraph of an article, and if they want more, they can keep reading. In a sense, then, everyone reads a different newspaper, for no two readers will read (or ignore) the same items.

But all television viewers see the same broadcast. They have no choices. A report is either in the broadcast or out, which means that anything which is of narrow interest is unlikely to be included. As NBC News executive Reuven Frank once explained:

A newspaper, for example, can easily afford to print an item of conceivable interest to only a fraction of its readers. A television news pro-

gram must be put together with the assumption
that each item will be of some interest to everyone that watches. Every time a newspaper includes a feature which will attract a specialized
group it can assume it is adding at least a little
bit to its circulation. To the degree a television
news program includes an item of this sort . . .
it must assume that its audience will diminish.

The need to "include everyone," an identifying feature
of commercial television in all its forms, prevents journalists from offering lengthy or complex explanations, or
from tracing the sequence of events leading up to today's
headlines. One of the ironies of political life in modern
democracies is that many problems which concern the
"general welfare" are of interest only to specialized
groups. Arms control, for example, is an issue that literally concerns everyone in the world, and yet the language of arms control and the complexity of the subject
are so daunting that only a minority of people can actually follow the issue from week to week and month to
month. If it wants to act responsibly, a newspaper can
at least make available more information about arms
control than most people want. Commercial television
cannot afford to do so.

But even if commercial television could afford to do
so, it wouldn't. The fact that television news is principally
made up of moving pictures prevents it from offering
lengthy, coherent explanations of events. A television

news show reveals the world as a series of unrelated, fragmentary moments. It does not—and cannot be expected to—offer a sense of coherence or meaning. What does this suggest to a TV viewer? That the viewer must come with a prepared mind—information, opinions, a sense of proportion, an articulate value system. To the TV viewer lacking such mental equipment, a news program is only a kind of rousing light show. Here a falling building, there a five-alarm fire, everywhere the world as an object, much without meaning, connections, or continuity.

9

THE

COMMERCIAL

The backbone, the heart, the soul, the fuel, the DNA (choose whatever metaphor you wish) of nonpublic television in America is the commercial. This is as true of the television news show as any other form of programming. To have a realistic understanding of TV news you must consider two dimensions of the commercial. The first concerns money; the second, social values.

Let's talk business, first, which means we must begin with the magic initials CPM. CPM is what makes the cash registers sing for news and other programs. It stands for cost per mil. Specifically, it is the cost to an advertiser for each thousand (mil) people reached by a commercial. When we last checked, the CPM of the "CBS Evening News" was approximately $5.10. That means an advertiser must spend $5.10 to reach each thousand people watching Dan Rather every weekday night. That works out to about half a cent for each viewer delivered, as counted by the rating services. The network, in effect, promises to deliver the audience but doesn't promise that any of them will watch the commercials or buy the products. If you step out of the room during the commercial to make a salami sandwich, and miss the commercial, the advertiser still gets charged. But with audiences in the millions, enough people see the commercials and buy enough products to make the system work.

Naturally, programs with high ratings (even if they have correspondingly high CPMs) are attractive to advertisers because they want to reach as many potential customers as possible at one time. News programs fill the bill. On any given weekday night, around thirty-eight million people are watching the network news, with millions more watching local news. About twelve million people watch morning news programs. For an advertiser who wants to reach a large audience, network news easily surpasses other news media, e.g., newspapers and magazines. The *Wall Street Journal* boasts the largest daily paper circulation, a little less than two million. *USA Today* is next with 1.33 million. *Time* magazine has a weekly circulation of 4.3 million people. Compare all that to the more than thirty-eight million people tuned to the ABC, CBS, and NBC news every weekday night.

But audience size is by no means the only factor advertisers are interested in. Even more important is demographics. Each news program has a demographic profile, that is, a statistical picture of the age, sex, and income of those who habitually watch the program. Advertisers of skateboards will tend to advertise on news programs with young viewers; advertisers of arthritis medicine would place their commercials on news programs with "older demographics."

It sounds simple enough but it isn't. Advertising agency spot buyers may have a difficult time trying to figure out where to spend the advertiser's dollar because a show with a small audience can make its news program a good "buy" by lowering its CPM. For example, as we write, ABC's "World News Tonight" is the number-one network news program with a nine rating (each rating point represents 1 percent of the 92.1 million households in the United States). Its cost per thousand is $5.64. But an advertiser shopping for a bargain might decide to spend the $5.10 CPM on the "CBS Evening News" with lower ratings, or the $5.46 CPM for the "NBC News with Tom Brokaw."

After those numbers have been carefully analyzed, spot buyers look at rate cards (which list the price of each news show's commercials) and make their decisions. On ABC news a thirty-second spot might cost $58,000; on NBC $50,700; on CBS $46,700. That's for thirty seconds of airtime. With about eight minutes of commercial time available each night, a network news show can generate about $400,000 a night, or $2 million each week. Moreover, because of the appeal of news shows, commercials placed adjacent to a news show will bring a premium price, as will commercials that lead in to local news programs. Where once there was one hour of news, local and network, many markets now feature two- and three-hour news programs. As we write, a countertrend is under way: reducing evening news program time in favor of double access, that is, one hour of syndicated shows preceding prime-time. Syndicated shows such as "Current Affair," "Wheel of Fortune," and "Entertainment Tonight" have replaced many locally produced news programs.

What all of this means is that the stakes in the ad game are astronomical. It is estimated that NBC, ABC, CBS, and Fox take in at least $4.5 billion a year in prime-time sales. It is estimated that each rating point is worth $8,000 for each thirty-second network commercial, but a commercial on a hit series can bring in $32,000 *more* per commercial than what is charged on an average series. That adds up to $224,000 *more* per week. The producer of the extremely successful "60 Minutes" news program, Don Hewitt, has boasted that his show makes $70 million a year for CBS (although industry figures estimate that the show earns only $40 million a year). It is generally believed that "20/20" brings in $20 million a year to ABC.

With so much money being spent just for airtime, advertisers and their agencies want their messages to be effective. To make sure that happens, advertisers bring in a small army of specialists, people who are experts in

making commercials. Over months of work, artists, stat-
isticians, writers, psychologists, researchers, musicians,
cinematographers, lighting consultants, camera operators, producers, directors, set builders, composers,
models, actors, audio experts, executives, and technicians
will toil for one single objective—to make a commercial
that will make you buy a product or idea. Time and
talent costs can be a half-million dollars for a short
commercial.

There are approximately 25,000 different commercials on network television every year. This is necessary,
in part, to keep pace with the two hundred or so new
items that appear every week on drugstore and super-
market shelves across the country. This means that advertisers have to produce commercials that will be
noticed and will motivate viewers to spend money. The
competition is fierce and continuous. At the same time,
the costs for advertisers have gotten so high that the sixty-
second commercial, once the backbone of broadcast TV,
has given way to shorter ten- and fifteen-second spots.
This "piggybacking" does bring the cost of each commercial down but it also squeezes four or more commercials into the same time slot that one commercial used
to fill. What this means is that next year, if you watch
TV as much as the average American, you will see something on the order of thirty thousand commercials, many
of them, of course, being repeats.

That number will include commercials that are part
of "line campaigns." These are commercials featuring

a whole line of products made by one company. For example, Colgate-Palmolive has made commercials that sold Colgate Junior toothpaste, regular Colgate toothpaste, Colgate anticavity mouth rinse, Colgate tartar-control toothpaste, and two kinds of Colgate tooth-brushes—all that in one sixty-second commercial. Companies favor the idea of "multipurpose" spots because they can sell several products for the cost of one commercial. Corporations also believe that the name of their company is as important a selling point as are the names of individual products. But it also means more ad clutter for the average viewer.

There is much more that can be said about the economics of commercials but what we *have* said, we believe, are the basics of the business. It is all about serious money. But commercials are also about the serious manipulation of our social and psychic lives. There are, in fact, some critics who say that commercials are a new albeit degraded means of religious expression in that most of them take the form of parables, teaching people what the good life consists of. It is a claim not to be easily dismissed. Let us take as an example an imaginary commercial for a mouthwash but one that replicates a common pattern. We'll call the product Fresh Taste. The commercial will run for thirty seconds, and, like any decent parable, will have a beginning, a middle, and an end. The beginning will show a man and woman saying good-bye at her door after an evening out. The woman tilts her head expecting to be kissed. The man steps back, in a state of polite revulsion, and says, "Well, Barbara, it was nice meeting you. I'll call sometime soon." Barbara is disappointed. And so ends Act I, which is accomplished in ten seconds. Act II shows Barbara talking to her room-mate. "This always happens to me, Joan," she laments. "What's wrong with me?" Joan is ready. "Your prob-lem," she says, "is with your mouthwash. Yours is too mediciny and doesn't protect you long enough. You should try Fresh Taste." Joan holds up a new bottle, which Barbara examines with an optimistic gleam in her eye. That's Act II. Also ten seconds. Act III, the final ten, shows Barbara and the once-reluctant young man getting off a plane in Hawaii. Both are in the early stages of ecstasy, and we are to understand that they are on their honeymoon. Fresh Taste has done it again.

Let's consider exactly what it *has* done. To begin with, the structure of the commercial is as compact and well-organized as the parable of the Prodigal Son, maybe even better organized and certainly more compressed. The first ten seconds show the problem: Barbara has trouble with her social life but is unaware of the cause. The second ten seconds show the solution: Barbara has bad breath, which could be remedied by her buying a different product. The last ten seconds show the moral of the story: if you know the right product to buy, you will find happiness.

Imagine, now, a slight alteration in the commercial. The first ten seconds remain the same. The change comes in Act II. Barbara wonders what's wrong with her but gets a somewhat different answer from Joan. "What's wrong with you?" Joan asks. "I'll tell you what's wrong with you. You are boring. You are dull, dull, dull. You haven't read a book in four years. You don't know the difference between Mozart and Bruce Springsteen. You couldn't even name the *continent* that Nigeria is on. It's a wonder that any man would want to spend more than ten minutes with you!" A chastened Barbara replies, "You are right. But what can I do?" "What can you do?" Joan answers. "I'll tell you what you can do. Start by taking a course or two at a local university. Join a book club. Get some tickets to the opera. Read *The New York Times* once in a while." "But that will take forever, months, maybe years," says Barbara. "That's right," replies Joan, "so you'd better start now." The commercial ends with Joan handing Barbara a copy of Freud's *Civilization and Its Discontents*. Barbara looks forlorn but begins to finger the pages.

This, too, is a parable but its lesson is so different from that of the first commercial that there is no chance you will ever see anything like it on television. Its point is that there are no simple or fast solutions to life's important problems; specifically, there is no chemical that can make you desirable: attractiveness must come from within. This idea, which is a commonplace in the Judeo-Christian tradition, is the exact opposite of what almost all commercials teach.

As we said, the average American TV viewer will see about thirty thousand commercials next year. Some of them are quite straightforward and some are funny, some are spoofs of other commercials and some are mysterious and exotic. But many of them will have the structure of our hypothetical commercial, and will urge the following ideas: Whatever problem you face (lack of self-esteem, lack of good taste, lack of attractiveness, lack of social acceptance), it can be solved, solved fast, and solved through a drug, a detergent, a machine, or a salable technique. You are, in fact, helpless unless you know about the product that can remake you and set you on the road to paradise. You must, in short, become a born-again consumer, redeem yourself, and find peace.

There are even commercials that show us a vision of hell should we fail to buy the right product. We are thinking, for example, of the American Express traveler's check commercial, which takes its symbolism straight from Dante's *Inferno*. The commercial shows a typical American couple checking out of a hotel in some strange city, perhaps Istanbul. The husband reaches for his wallet but cannot find it. He has lost it, along with his traveler's checks. The check-out clerk asks, with hope in his eyes, if the lost checks were American Express traveler's checks, for if they are, they are easily enough replaced. The husband, his voice practically gone, says they are not. The clerk shrugs his shoulders, as if to say, "Then, there is no hope for you." Perhaps you have seen this commercial. Have you ever wondered what happens to these people? Do they wander forever in limbo? Will they always be in an alien land far from home? Will they ever see their children again? Is this not a just punishment for their ignorance, for their lack of attention? The truth, after all, was available to them. Why were they not able to see it?

Perhaps you are thinking we exaggerate. After all, most people don't pay all that much attention to commercials. But that, in fact, is one of the reasons commercials are so effective. People do not usually *analyze* them. Neither, we might say, do people analyze biblical parables, which are often ambiguous; some, as in the case of the parable of the Prodigal Son, seem even downright unfair. Like biblical parables, commercial messages invade our consciousness, seep into our souls. Even if you are half-awake when commercials run, thirty thousand of them will begin to penetrate your indifference. In the end, it is hard not to believe.

Whether you call the structure and messages of commercials "religious," "quasi-religious," "anti-religious," or something else, it is clear that they are the most constant and voluminous source of value propaganda in our culture. Commercials are almost never about anything trivial. Mouthwash commercials are not about bad breath. They are about the need for social acceptance and, frequently, about the need to be sexually attractive. Beer commercials are almost always about a man's need to share the values of a peer group. An automobile commercial is usually about the need for autonomy or social status, a deodorant commercial about one's fear of nature. Television commercials are about products only in the sense that the story of Jonah is about the anatomy of whales, which is to say, they aren't. Like the story of Jonah, they set out to teach us lessons about the solutions to life's problems, and that is why we are inclined to think of them as a corrupt modality of spiritual instruction.

Boredom, anxiety, rejection, fear, envy, sloth—in TV commercials there are remedies for each of these, and more. The remedies are called Scope, Comet, Toyota, Bufferin, Alka-Seltzer, and Budweiser. They take the place of good works, restraint, piety, awe, humility, and transcendence. On TV commercials, moral deficiencies as we customarily think of them do not really exist. A commercial for Alka-Seltzer, for example, does not teach you to avoid overeating. Gluttony is perfectly acceptable—maybe even desirable. The point of the commercial is that your gluttony is no problem. Alka-Seltzer will handle it. The Seven Deadly Sins, in other words, are problems to be solved through chemistry and technology. On commercials, there are no intimations of the conventional roads to spiritual redemption. But there is Original Sin, and it consists of our having been ignorant of a product that offers happiness. We may achieve a state of grace by attending to the good news about it, which will appear every six or seven minutes. It follows from this that he or she is most devout who knows of the largest array of products; they are heretics who willfully ignore what is there to be used.

Part of the reason commercials are effective is that

they are, in a sense, invisible. When you check the TV listings in your local newspaper or *TV Guide*, do you find the commercials listed? Since there will be eight minutes of commercials in a thirty-minute news show, would it not be relevant to indicate what the content of 27 percent of the show will be? But, of course, the commercials will not be listed. They are simply taken for granted, which is why so few people regard it as strange that a commercial should proceed a news story about an earthquake in Chile, or, even worse, *follow* a news story about an earthquake in Chile. It is difficult to measure the effect on an audience that has been shown pictures of an earthquake's devastation, and immediately afterward is subjected to commercials for Gleem toothpaste, Scope, United Airlines, and Alka-Seltzer. Our best guess is that the earthquake takes on a surrealistic aspect; it is certainly trivialized. It is as if the program's producer is saying, "You needn't grieve or worry about what you are seeing. In a minute or so, we will make you happy with some good news about how to make your teeth whiter."

Of course, an argument may be made that a concern over how to make your teeth whiter is far more important than your lamentations about an earthquake; that is to say, advertising fuels a capitalist economy. For a market economy to work, the population must be made to believe that it is in need of continuous improvement. If you are quite satisfied with your teeth, your hair, your 1987 Honda, and your weight, you will not be an avid consumer. Especially will you be worthless to the economy if your mind is preoccupied with worldly events. If you are not an avid consumer, the engine of the economy slows and then stalls. Therefore, the thematic thrust of advertising is to take your mind off earthquakes, the homeless, and other irrelevancies, and get you to think about your inadequate self and how you can get better. Of course, the traditional point of journalism is to turn you away from yourself and toward the world. Thus in the intermingling of news and commercials we have a struggle of sorts between two different orientations. Each tries to refute the other. It will be interesting to know which point of view will triumph in the long run.

10

TELEVISION
IN THE
COURTROOM

We would not be surprised if many Americans believe that if something is not on a television news show, it isn't news—or at least not important news. Some may also believe that anything and everything *ought* to be on television. Many television journalists come close to believing that, and usually defend their view by mumbling something about "the public's right to know." How much the "public" has a right to know, and when and why and how, are, in fact, troubling questions. Does the "public" have a right, for example, to see and hear what goes on in a Confessional box? Of course not, most will say. That is strictly a private matter between a priest and a sinner. Well, then, does the "public" have a right to see and hear what goes on in a public school classroom, which, after all, is supported by tax dollars? Some would say "yes," provided that the visitor's presence does not interfere with the lesson. But everyone can't get into a classroom. How about televising the lesson so that everyone has access to what's going on there? And what if the teacher objects? Or the students? Should they be permitted to bar a television camera to their classroom? Some would say "yes." What happens between teacher and students is at least a quasi-private matter, and the "public" ought not to be forced upon them. Some would say "no." The "public" pays for the school, the teachers, and everything else related to the enterprise. If it wants cameras there, cameras should be there—whether or not teachers and students object. It is a tricky issue but somewhat irrelevant since almost nobody is *that* interested in classrooms, least of all television journalists.

But as for courtrooms, that is a different matter. Many people are fascinated by courtrooms, as evidenced by the success of representations from "Perry Mason" to Judge Wapner to "L.A. Law." Television news directors and producers are well aware of this fascination, and almost universally favor the idea of televising actual trials. Televised trials make for good television, which means large audiences, which means higher rates for commercials, which probably means better salary deals when contracts are negotiated. Besides, many television journalists say, the "public" has a right to know.

We have put the word "public" in quotation marks because it has a somewhat ambiguous meaning, especially in the context of the dispute about the appropriateness of televising actual courtroom trials. There are, in fact, two meanings to the word "public" that are quite different from each other. The first meaning is, simply, the opposite of secret or private. In America and other civilized countries trials are always public in that journalists, interested parties, and ordinary citizens have access to the proceedings. There is nothing secret about the matter except in those instances where a judge confers "privately" with opposing counsels on some technical legal issue. The other meaning of "public" refers to a huge, undifferentiated audience—the proverbial man and woman in the street who may or may not have an interest in what journalists believe it is their right to know. Everyone, we assume, is in favor of keeping trials public (in the sense of the first meaning). But not everyone agrees that the "public" (in its second meaning) has a right to see trials on television.

To get to the heart of the matter, we must provide a short history of the controversy, which began with the invention and development of photography in the midnineteenth century. At that point, it became possible to provide citizens with a view of the American court system never before witnessed except by the tiny minority who had actually been in courts. But from the outset, there were concerns expressed that the presence of still cameras in the courts would be an intrusion on the proceedings, and damage the dignity if not the sanctity of the courts. Many jurists believed that the purpose of a trial was not to inform or educate the public but to conduct a rigorous search for truth, and that court proceedings were designed to do just that. A camera, they believed, was an unnecessary addition to the judicial environment.

In 1917 the Illinois State Supreme Court became the first legal authority to advise state courts to bar cameras during trials. Until this decision, photojournalists had access to Illinois courts, although granting such access was left to the discretion of each judge. In 1925 forty-five Chicago judges voted to prohibit cameras in state courtrooms during judicial proceedings. Nonetheless, in other parts of the country, judges were of mixed opinion about the appropriateness of allowing cameras in the courts. One of the most famous decisions in favor of having them was made by Judge John T. Raulston, who presided at the "monkey" trial of John Scopes in Dayton, Tennessee, in 1925. News photographers were allowed to take photographs during certain moments of the trial, including photographs of Clarence Darrow addressing the court. Radio broadcasts were also made from the court, and the general atmosphere was far from dignified. Nonetheless, judicial opinion about the use of cameras still remained divided after the Scopes trial. In a Maryland murder case that followed two years later, a trial judge cited two photographers and three editors from Baltimore's *News* and *American* for contempt after discovering that seven photographs had been taken surreptitiously during the first day of the trial. Two of the photographs were published the following day. The newspapers argued that while the judge had discretionary power, he could not ban cameras completely. But a court of appeals decision concluded that a judge could act to limit and even prohibit cameras in order to protect a defendant's rights and to maintain judicial decorum. The newspapers were forced to pay a fine of $5,000 and the five newsmen were sentenced to one day in jail.

The Maryland decision, however, did not settle the issue. The matter was decided, or so it seemed, in 1935 by the trial of Bruno Hauptmann, accused of kidnapping and murdering the baby of Charles and Anne Morrow Lindbergh. At that trial, in Flemington, New Jersey, Judge Thomas Trenchard allowed the use of both newsreel and still photography within the courtroom although under some restrictions. For example, no filming was permitted when the judge was seated on the bench but witnesses could repeat highlights of their testimony to photojournalists following court proceedings.

It is generally believed that the presence of photographers turned the courtroom into a circus, one newsman calling the scene "a Roman Holiday." At one point, over-zealous photographers made the judge decide to bar all photographic coverage in the courtroom. Ironically, a hidden newsreel camera took footage that was later shown in movie theaters all over the country.

As a result of the Hauptmann trial, the American Bar Association formed a special committee to study the issue. The committee urged a ban on cameras, expressed in a recommendation that came to be known as Canon

35. Canons of the American Bar Association do not carry
with them the force of law, but this one became the basis
of legislation aimed at banning still and newsreel cameras, and later, in 1952, TV cameras, from the courts.
State legislatures, one after the other, codified the canon
into state law so that by 1965 all states except Colorado
and Texas had such laws. In fact, the first live TV broadcast of a trial took place in Waco, Texas, on December 6,
1955. The judge, of course, approved but so did the jury
and even the defendant, who was being tried for murder.
The state of Colorado was equally lenient about cameras,
and as a result of a petition by media representatives con-
cerning the case of John Gilbert Graham (he was being
tried for planting a bomb on an airplane, which killed
forty-four people, including his mother), the court
worked out an agreement that permitted cameras entry
but with stations "pooling" their resources. Colorado, in
fact, became the first state to allow TV cameras in state
courtrooms with the permission of the presiding judge.

The traditional argument against allowing cameras
in the courts was that they were, by their nature, intru-
sive; that is, they were distracting and noisy. These arguments weakened as media technologies improved, and,
especially, as TV technology became less physically cum-
bersome. However, other arguments began to surface.
For example, it was claimed that the presence of cameras
could create psychological problems for judges, lawyers,
witnesses, and juries. The argument for allowing cameras
in the courts continued along the same lines used from

the beginning: the press had an absolute right to cover trials as guaranteed by the First Amendment, and to do so by using whatever tools of the trade were available. Thus, a constitutional conflict arose between a defendant's right to a fair trial and the First Amendment right of a free press. The American Bar Association tended toward the view that the defendant's rights outweighed the rights of the press and, in 1965, received support from a decision by the U.S. Supreme Court in the case of *Estes* v. *Texas*. Billy Sol Estes was a prominent political figure who had been convicted in a Texas courtroom in 1962 for fraudulent financial dealings. The trial judge, as was the predisposition in Texas courts, allowed photographers and TV cameras into the courtroom during pretrial hearings. The U.S. Supreme Court reversed Estes's conviction on the grounds that the televising of "notorious criminal trials" was a denial of the defendant's right to due process. In addition to citing the fact that the cameras had been a distraction, the Court, in a five to four ruling, made a broad condemnation of television claiming that the use of in-court cameras was itself unfriendly to the judicial process. The Court claimed cameras could corrupt a juror's impartiality, impair the testimony of witnesses, affect a judge's decisions, and subject the defendant to mental harassment.

But the continuing insistence of the press that it was being denied its constitutional rights kept the door ajar. In 1977 the state of Florida broke the door down. In that year, a pilot project was begun, under the auspices of the State Supreme Court, allowing trials to be televised. Among the trials included in the pilot project was that of Ronny Zamora, a fifteen-year-old charged with murdering an eighty-two-year-old woman. The trial received national attention, not only because it was televised but also because of Zamora's defense. He had been made insane, he claimed, by watching violent television programs. Presiding judge Paul Baker, who had originally been opposed to the pilot project, concluded by the end of the trial that the pilot experiment was a success, that is, it demonstrated that the courts and the electronic press can work harmoniously. The tide began to turn. In fact, in the following year, the U.S. Supreme Court, in effect, reversed itself on *Estes*. Two former Miami Beach policemen who had been found guilty of burglary, Noel Chandler and Robert Granger, appealed their conviction, arguing that the presence of TV cameras at their trial influenced the behavior of attorneys, witnesses, and jurors. They relied heavily on the Court's reasoning in *Estes* but it didn't work. A considerable number of legal organizations, state chief justices, and state attorneys general filed briefs with the Court, maintaining that cameras in no way harmed the judicial process. The Supreme Court agreed, as did many state legislatures throughout the country. By the time *Chandler* v. *Florida* was decided, twenty-nine states had adopted rules allowing cameras on either a permanent or experimental basis. By April 1987, forty-three states had some form of rules permitting camera coverage during trials (although only twenty-seven states allowed coverage of criminal trials).

In December 1987, New York became the forty-fourth state to allow TV cameras into the courtroom. When the relevant law expired, cameras were barred from the courts. A serious debate on the matter continued for almost five years. As of this writing, state legislators have reached an agreement that would again allow TV cameras in the state's courtrooms, but with new restrictions intended to protect witnesses in criminal trials. This debate has relevance beyond New York State. Keep in mind that in 1965 (the *Estes* case) it appeared that cameras would be permanently barred from most courtrooms. That changed but it can change again.

Because of our familiarity with the arguments, we can summarize the case for and against cameras in the courts. (One of us, Postman, was a member of the New York State Advisory Committee on Cameras in the Courts, whose function was to assess the competing evidence and points of view on the matter. Powers has used trial footage in his TV news stories.) Here's the way it stacks up:

1. Journalists and TV executives, especially of news departments, claim that the First Amendment to the Constitution gives them an absolute right to be in the courtroom with their cameras, provided, of course, that the cameras in no way disrupt the proceedings. If the print press can be there, the electronic press can be there. It is even questionable that the electronic press has to await *permission* from a state legislature in order to gain entry.

This, the argument goes, is none of the legislature's business. The First Amendment makes that clear. The only question to be decided is whether or not the cameras are a distraction. In the days of Hauptmann and even *Estes*, they might have been. But now a camera is only part of the furniture and is completely unobtrusive.

The reply to this argument usually begins with the word "nonsense." It goes on from there as follows: From 1927, when Congress passed the Radio Act, to 1934, when the Federal Communications Act was passed, to the present, Congress and the courts have distinguished between print and broadcasting. Unlike a newspaper, which is *owned* by a person or corporation, a TV channel cannot be owned by anyone. The airwaves belong to the people, who lease a frequency, and who can revoke or otherwise deny a lease if the broadcaster does not operate the station in "the public interest, convenience, and necessity." *The New York Times*, for example, is not required to publish in the public interest, does not require a government license, and is not legally responsible to the "people." A TV station is. Therefore, the First Amendment does not give the electronic press absolute protection against government regulation or restrictions. If a legislature wishes to bar TV cameras from the courts, it may do so.

As for the question of the camera's intrusiveness, the evidence is not as clear as TV executives claim. It is difficult to know exactly how the presence of a TV camera alters the behavior of participants in a trial. Some research suggests that changes in behavior are minimal; a few studies indicate that both witnesses and lawyers are demonstrably affected by the presence of cameras. The argument against cameras claims that Chief Justice Earl Warren (in *Estes*) was right: any time you put cameras into a situation, you change the situation. Only further, more detailed, and more sophisticated research can tell us to what extent the situation is changed.

2. Those in favor of cameras in the courts also argue that television has enormous potential for educating the "public" (in the second meaning of the word). Surveys of the public's knowledge of the judicial system consistently reveal that most people know very little about the judicial process. One study uncovered the astonishing fact that roughly one-third of those people who had *served on juries* did not know that a defendant is considered innocent until proven guilty. Such ignorance is unacceptable in a democratic society, and whatever can be done to eradicate it should be done. Television is an indispensable medium for enlarging public understanding of an essential institution.

The educational value of televising trials was stressed in the preamble to New York's law in 1987. The hope was expressed that the televising of trials would not only increase the public's knowledge of the courts but would also increase respect for the judicial process.

The reply to this is as follows: it doesn't. The one study we know of that bears on the issue (by Dr. William Petkanas of New York University) reveals that after eighteen months of televised trials on New York State TV stations, the audience knew no more about the operation of the courts, and had no greater respect for the judicial process, than before trials were televised. The usual explanation for this is that TV stations never show a trial in its entirety. In fact, they usually show a thirty- or sixty-second fragment of a trial, most often a dramatic moment. One of the ironic discoveries of the Petkanas study is that fictionalized trials (in "L.A. Law," for example) seem to educate the public better than do actual trials. For example, most people in the survey knew that a defense lawyer is an "officer of the court." When queried as to how they knew this, most said that the fact is frequently mentioned on lawyer shows.

One reply to the failure of TV to increase knowledge of the courts is that education takes time. The cumulative effect of the public's seeing even fragments of trials will be demonstrable years from now, and cannot be detected in a short period.

3. Another argument for including cameras is that our public institutions must learn to accommodate themselves to new technologies. It is reactionary and regressive to pretend that television does not exist. We cannot turn the clock back. Schools, businesses, theaters, the halls of Congress, political conventions, even ballparks have made adjustments to fit new technological possibilities. So must the courts.

In fact, over the centuries, the courts have done this. There was a time when law was entirely based on the oral tradition. With the invention of writing, then printing, law changed. Judges decide cases on the basis of *written precedent*. Lawyers' briefs are written documents. The courts have always reconceived their rules to exploit the advantages of new media of communication. Photographs are admitted as evidence; so are wiretaps and other recordings. In other words, the judicial process has never been indifferent to technological progress. Why stop television from doing what it can do?

Moreover, until recently the courts were largely a semipublic space, available only to those who could be physically present. Television converts the courts into public space. It doesn't matter if the public is "educated" or not by televised trials any more than it matters if the public is educated by seeing a televised press conference or political convention. Television is a window to the world. People will enjoy seeing that world or not, will learn from it or not. But it is there, and it makes no sense to say we will pull down the shades when it comes to trials.

The answer to these arguments is as follows: First, what's wrong with turning back the clock if the clock is wrong? We need not be slaves to our technologies. Every technological advance has its advantages and disadvantages. It is our job to control the uses of technology so that what is best about our culture can be preserved. Second, television does not turn trials into a public event but into a public spectacle. Let's be honest about this: what the public is shown is intended only to entertain them, even titillate them. TV stations are not, in fact,

interested in showing trials but only in showing fragments of "sexy" trials, those that involve murder, rape,
kidnapping, and other horrifying crimes. TV stations
would, if they could, show the actual murders, rapes, and
kidnappings themselves. In fact, as of this writing, a San
Francisco TV station is petitioning to be allowed to televise an execution. Why? Not because it is good public
policy, we suspect, but only because it would draw a
huge audience. But failing to televise actual deaths, TV
must settle for the next best "show"—a glimpse of a
murderer on trial. The whole trial won't be shown because much of it is too complex for the audience, and
complexity always leads to an indifferent audience.

As for the courtroom being a semipublic space, that's
exactly what it should be. Its rules have been worked out
over centuries. The procedures are not perfect but they
are designed to give everyone a fair shake, and there is
no good reason to alter them. And keep this in mind:
reading about a trial and seeing it on television are two
quite different experiences. A man who is found not guilty
ordinarily may resume his life. A man who is found not
guilty but who has been seen on television during his
trial may find it impossible to resume his life. Audiences
may even forget if he was found guilty or not. In any
case, he becomes notorious in one way or another, which
is to say, he is tried twice—once in the courts, and a
second time in the court of public exposure.

As of this moment, the trend is entirely toward allowing cameras in the courts. Even in New York, which

forbids cameras, we can expect permission to be granted soon, provided that certain rules are put in place—possibly, that defendants must agree to allow the use of cameras. We shall see. Meanwhile, the cameras are there in most places, including a cable service, Court TV, which features trials. The "hot" trial of the moment is featured with anchors/commentators guiding us through the proceedings. Critics fear that Court TV, in aiming for a wide general audience, will focus on the sensational, thus trivializing the court system. Our own view is that opening the courtroom to the television eye might increase public understanding of the judicial system, but only if coverage extends beyond TV's need to dramatize the moment.

11

WHAT
DOES IT ALL
MEAN?

In coming toward the end of our book, we must address the question that is the title of this chapter. We will begin by saying something about children. No book about television—*any* aspect of television—can neglect doing that, since it is generally assumed that children are more vulnerable to what may be confusing, destructive, or enriching about television than adults. This assumption may not be valid but there is no denying that children are the most avid group of TV viewers. In America, those between the ages of two and twelve watch an average of twenty-five hours of television per week. The young ones watch about five thousand hours before entering the first grade; and by high school's end the average American youngster has clocked nineteen thousand hours in front of a TV set. The same youngster will have spent only thirteen thousand hours in school, assuming that he or she is regular in attendance. What it comes down to is that American children spend 30 percent of their waking hours in front of a television set. And that means exposure to roughly thirteen thousand killings, about 100,000 violent episodes, and somewhere in the neighborhood of 650,000 commercials.

Given all this, it can come as no surprise, to say the least, that our youngsters know more about Dr. Huxtable than Dr. Zhivago, and that their heads are full of jingles about McDonald's, Coca-Cola, and Teenage Mutant Ninja Turtles. It should be noted, by the way, that 30 percent of the commercials on children's programs are for food, including breakfast cereals, candy, soft drinks, and other sugary products. If our children know more about munchies and crunchies than about how much protein they need for healthy nutrition every day, no one need be astonished.

For quite a long time, scholars have attempted to discover exactly what effects television has on our young. Because television is by no means the only factor influencing the minds of our youth, it is not easy to pin this down. Some studies indicate that children who watch a lot of TV tend to spend less time outdoors, and don't play with friends as much as children who are light viewers. In its 1990 policy statement, the American Academy of Pediatrics concluded that too much TV can make children fat since TV viewing is a sedentary activity.

There are even some studies indicating that children who view a lot of television do less well in school than light viewers. One of the more comprehensive recent studies, supported by the National Institute of Mental Health, is worth mentioning. The investigators, Robert Kubey of Rutgers University and Mihaly Csikszentmihalyi (pronounced Schwartz) of the University of Chicago, were not primarily interested in TV's effects on children but uncovered enough data to lead them to suggest that children be educated in the art of TV watching so that they will be less easily manipulated. Their research spanned thirteen years, and involved twelve hundred subjects in nine different studies. Their conclusion: television makes people passive, tense, and unable to concentrate; more skill and concentration are required in the act of eating than in watching television; although people assume that TV watching offers relaxation and escape, it actually leaves people in worse moods than they were in before watching television.

There are, of course, many studies focusing on the effects of TV violence on children—at last count about three thousand—many of them ambiguous. Nonetheless, after reviewing the data, the American Academy of Pediatrics concluded that TV violence "promotes a proclivity to violence and a passive response to its practice." Which brings us to TV news.

TV news is now more accessible to children than ever. News shows are on the air from early morning until late at night and there is no lack of realism depicting the violence in the human condition. Rapes, muggings, terrorism, and drug-related murders and kidnappings are the currency of the evening news. And with the proliferation of pseudo-news tabloid shows, young eyes can feast on wall-to-wall horror, and the horror can feast on young minds. During "sweeps" periods (when a television station has its audience measured), sordid subjects of every known variety, and a few that were previously unknown, are wheeled out, advertised, and featured to attract an audience. The audience includes children. Here we come to the heart of a major problem. By contrast with other media (e.g., books, newspapers, magazines), television is an "open-admission" technology. It does not require reading skills. It is largely free. It is activated by a turn of a switch. Its programs are designed to gratify emotions immediately. It is more than friendly to its users. It adores them. As a consequence, the six-year-old and the sixty-year-old are equally vulnerable to what TV has to offer. Television, in this sense, is the consummate egalitarian medium of communication, surpassing oral language itself. For in speaking, we may always whisper so that the children will not hear. Or we may use words they may not understand. But television cannot whisper, and its pictures are concrete and vivid. The children see everything TV reveals.

The most obvious effect of this situation is that it eliminates the exclusivity of worldly knowledge. This means that the knowledge that distinguishes adults from children, that is, the "secrets" of adult life—political secrets, sexual secrets, medical secrets, and so on—are now constantly in view, including the extent to which human beings are prone to violence. In an earlier time, it was possible, within limits, to keep this knowledge from children, which was done for a perfectly good reason: too much of such knowledge, too soon, is considered dangerous to the well-being of an unformed mind. Enlightened opinion on child development claims it is necessary for children to believe that adults have control over their impulses to violence and have a clear conception of right and wrong. Through these beliefs children develop positive feelings about themselves that give them strength to nurture their rationality, which, in turn, will sustain them in adversity. But TV undermines this entire process. And here we must keep in mind that the stylized murders, rapes, and plunderings that are depicted on weekly fictional programs are much less than half the problem. Such programs are, after all, understood to be fiction or pseudo—fairy tales, and we may assume (although not safely) that some children do not take them to be representations of real adult life. Far more significant are the daily examples of violence and moral degeneracy that are the staple of TV news shows. These are not mitigated by the presence of recognizable and attractive actors and actresses. They are put forward as the stuff of everyday life. These are real murders, real rapes, real plunderings. And the fact that they *are* the stuff of real life makes them all the more powerful.

What are the long-range effects on children of their

seeing mayhem and adult incompetence every night on TV news? No one can be sure. Some say that the effect may be positive in that children will develop a more realistic sense of what life is like. The argument is made that the traditional manner of socializing children is hypocritical. We do not live in a Mary Poppins world, and the sooner children know this, the better. But it seems to us that hypocrisy should be made of sterner stuff. If it is hypocrisy to conceal from children the "facts" of adult violence and moral ineptitude, it is nonetheless wise to do so. Surely, hypocrisy in the cause of fostering healthy psychological development in children is no vice.

But it is probably useless to debate this issue. The plain facts are these: television operates around the clock, its audiences cannot be segregated, and programs, especially TV news, require a continuous supply of novel information to engage the audience. Thus television must make use of every existing taboo in the culture, including sexual perversity, irrational violence, insanity, and the ineptitude of political leaders. Taboos may be discussed on talk shows, soap operas, commercials, or news shows. How the information comes is irrelevant. Television needs material, for its business is to *move* information, not collect it. And as long as the present system of competitive, commercial broadcasting exists, this situation will also exist. We suspect that if every network executive and program director were replaced tomorrow by, say, the faculty of the Harvard Divinity School, TV programming, including TV news shows, would remain quite close to what it is.

One might think, therefore, that in the face of this some attempts would be made to shield children from news shows, or at least to provide them with a different vision of the news. In fact, there have been some attempts to design TV news specifically for children. At least two have been beamed right into the classroom. Turner Broadcasting produces a fifteen-minute news program for children called "CNN Newsroom," and it comes without commercial interruption. On the other hand, "Channel One," produced by Whittle Communications, a unit of Time-Warner Inc., presents newscasts complete with commercials. Participating schools are given fifty thousand dollars' worth of TV monitors, VCRs, and a satellite dish in exchange for requiring students to watch the program. The show consists of ten minutes of news and two minutes of commercials. The four thirty-second spots cost advertisers $150,000 each. "Channel One" has been banned by some states, including New York and California, on the grounds that it exploits children under the guise of presenting an educational program. The claim is made that the shows are too simplistic, are too fast-paced to allow much development, and are merely cynical attempts to take advantage of gullible children. Other educators claim that news shows in the classroom make civics lessons come alive and open the door to interesting classroom discussions. The former president of Action for Children's Television, Peggy Charren, has criticized "Channel One" for encouraging consumerism in teenagers even while they are in a learning environment. Whittle Communications, of course, defends its newscasts and notes that newspapers and magazines that carry advertising are routinely used in schools; even soda machines in schools are advertisements of sorts.

While it is true that the school environment is not a "commercial-free" zone, the question remains: should the students be "for sale" to the highest bidder? The stakes are high. "Channel One" claims it will reach six million students by the end of 1991. That translates into hundreds of millions of advertising dollars.

Apparently, there will be no relief from the news wherever we go, and that leads us to a problem that all of us must face, not only children. One way to express the problem is by recalling a remark made by the American novelist Philip Roth. In commenting on the difference between being a novelist in the West and being a novelist behind the Iron Curtain (this was before the collapse of Communism in Eastern Europe), Roth said that in Eastern Europe nothing is permitted but everything matters; with us, everything is permitted but nothing matters. The observation may no longer apply to the work of novelists but it does apply to the news business. We have here, in other words, a paradox of sorts. The more information, the less significant information is. The less information, the more significant it is. There is nothing so unusual about this. Perhaps it is a law of human nature. To a man with fifty suits, one suit is not so important. To a man with one suit, that suit is everything. We are, of course, not making an argument for denying people access to information. But we are calling attention to the problem known as information glut. Put simply, it is this: as our news media, especially television, fill our days with information from everywhere, about everything, we have increasing difficulty in deciding what any of it means. We do not have time to reflect on any piece of news, and we are rarely helped, least of all by television itself, to know what weight or value to assign to any of it. We become information junkies, addicted to news, demanding (even requiring) more and more of it but without any notion of what to do with it.

Television, we need to say, did not start all this. The roots of information glut are to be found in the mid-nineteenth century with the invention of the telegraph and photograph. There followed, over the next century, a dazzling demonstration of technological ingenuity that gave us the rotary press, radio, the telephone, motion pictures, and computers, in addition to television. This development is usually called "the communications revolution," sometimes "the information explosion." Marshall McLuhan, the first "media guru" of our age, claimed that the electronic world in which we now live has created a "global village," in which everything has become everyone's business. McLuhan probably never lived in a village; if he had, he might have used a different metaphor for our present situation. In a village, information is apt to be a precious commodity. Villagers seek information that directly affects their lives, and they usually know what to do with it when they get it. Villagers may like gossip, as it adds a certain zest to life, but they usually can distinguish between what is gossip and what materially affects their lives. Our relation to information is quite different. For us, information is a commodity. It is bought and sold. Most of it has little to do with our lives. And most of the time, we don't know what to do with it.

We can, of course, use information as entertainment, as, for example, during the Gulf War. Viewers were witnesses to the first attack on Baghdad, as the U.S. and other U.N. forces launched their offensive. Ironically, this amazing television first was in audio form only, as journalists in their hotel rooms telephoned their reports to CNN in Atlanta. Subsequently, satellite uplinks brought the war into living rooms around the world. Network correspondents covering the war were admonished not to give too much detail about the ensuing battles because the information might help the enemy, who was watching television, too. Many Americans got out of their beds at 4:00 A.M. eastern standard time to watch the noon briefings in Saudi Arabia. The commander of the allied forces, General Norman Schwarzkopf, showed videos of "smart bombs" and described battle strategies, thus allowing viewers to know exactly and at the same instant what the reporters covering the briefings could know. Viewers also witnessed the seriocomic scenes of TV reporters diving for cover as air raid sirens went off during their stand-ups. Viewers saw live reports as Kuwait City was liberated, heard incoming Scud missile attacks on Israel and Saudi Arabia, and watched as Iraqis surrendered and the wounded were brought to hospitals. The eyewitness video lens made newspapers stale with their day-old coverage.

All of this, you will remember, was presented as a kind of show, a drama that entertained as much as anything else. There were heroes and villains; there were acts and scenes. Each network, incredibly, had a theme song to introduce news about the war ("The Desert Song"?). The play had a name—in fact, two names. First, Desert Shield, then Desert Storm. We came to the war as we would a mini-series, and, as it turned out, a good one, at that. The last act was entirely satisfactory, allowing for parades celebrating the glorious return of the warriors. General Schwarzkopf has been able to retire as a millionaire, with a book contract and, of course, a lucrative career as a TV commentator and lecturer.

As we write, the revels are over, and most people are no longer interested. We do not say, by the way, that the war was unjustified. That would be the subject of a different book. We are saying that television tends to turn its news into a form of entertainment, in part because so much information is available that news has lost its relevance and meaning; that is, Americans are no longer clear about what news is worth remembering or how any of it is connected to anything else. As a consequence, Americans have rapidly become the least knowledgeable people in the industrialized world. We know *of* many things (everything is revealed) but *about* very little (nothing is known).

As this chapter was being written, the National Council of Educational Standards and Testing was holding conferences to design school programs that would meet "world-class standards." American students are several tiers below students in other countries in intellectual achievement, as well as historical knowledge, and no one, apparently, knows why. It has not yet occurred to our education leaders that our students, like the rest of us, are suffering from information glut. They do not yet acknowledge that it is impossible to read the writing on a wall if, every day, new words are written over the old ones. The writing soon loses its coherence and becomes a jumble. After a while, the wall may become an object of aesthetic contemplation; people may enjoy looking at it but it will be worthless as a medium of rational expression, that is, as a means of organizing one's knowledge.

There are some critics and scholars who take a different view of all this. For example, Henry Perkinson, in his *Getting Better: Television and Moral Progress*, believes that the proliferation of images, especially on television news shows, tends to make viewers more sensitive to the sufferings of other people. Television news allowed us to see, for example, the face of the enemy during the Vietnam War; it showed us the pain and humiliation of blacks being beaten in our own country, of students being shot in China, of children starving in Ethiopia, of Russians resisting an illegal coup. The cumulative effect of all this has been to widen our moral universe, and connect us emotionally with people who, before television, were merely abstract "others." In his book, Perkinson provides examples of what he sees as an historical evolution of morals, as humankind has progressed from speech to writing to printing to television. We recommend his book, especially to those who are chronically depressed. As for us, we find the evidence for moral improvement difficult to find, and when found, even more difficult to believe.

We would respond in the same way to the contention that the images provided by TV news serve to bind the nation and provide a sense of national purpose. There is no denying that funerals of political leaders, scenes of hostages being released, the horrific vision of astronauts being blown out of the sky, the joy or anguish of a ground ball slipping through the legs of a Red Sox first-baseman are fixed in the consciousness of American TV viewers. These events and their accompanying imagery certainly provide us with material for conversation but it is not yet demonstrable that shared images make for shared purposes or even shared understandings. In fact, a quite opposite trend is under way. We refer to the return to "tribalism," as different ethnic, racial, and religious groups aggressively reject the metaphor of the "melting pot." They insist on the supremacy of their unique identities, and demand that our social, political, and educational systems recognize the reality of "multicul-

turalism." In other words, if TV's images have enriched
our sense of a national heritage, it is not yet manifest.

We take no pleasure in seeming so pessimistic. That
television, and in particular TV news, might be an in-
tellectually enriching and morally ennobling enterprise
is devoutly to be wished—by us, as well as anyone else.
Who knows? It might yet be. But we are trying to be
realistic, and such optimism as we have is reserved for
the next and final chapter, where we indicate what you
may do to defend yourself against the negative influence
of TV news, and to maximize what is useful.

12

WHAT
CAN YOU DO?

Below we have listed eight recommendations, with accompanying commentaries, which you may find useful in adjusting your relation to TV news shows, or in helping others to do so. We have not included among them the most effective strategy, which is to move to Switzerland. Some people have thought of this but the Swiss are very particular about who they let in, so it is impractical. Those recommendations that follow are, we believe, well within the competence of anyone who has come this far in our book.

1.

*In encountering a news show,
you must come with a firm idea
of what is important.*

Even an "open mind" has to have boundaries, and you
will be endlessly manipulated if you have no clear basis
for evaluating the significance of "news." Remember: TV
news is not what happened. It is what some man or
woman who has been labeled a "journalist" or "correspondent" thinks is worth reporting. You may agree or
not but it is *your* business to judge the importance of
what is reported. Journalists would prefer you to trust
them. Walter Cronkite did a disservice to viewers by
concluding his famous CBS nightly news program with
the words, "And that's the way it was on this day . . ."
What he meant to say, and should have said, is, "And
that's the way our gang on Fifty-seventh Street thought
things were on this day . . ."

We suggest that if you form your own notions of
what is worth reporting, you will not be so easily manipulated by the choices of TV news directors and journalists. Of course, the question of how one develops a
sense of what is significant is very complex, well beyond
the scope of our book and also beyond our competence.
But, obviously, family background and, especially, education play an important role here. If we were to write
a book on education, we would certainly stress the point

that our schools have apparently abandoned the task of helping youngsters construct a moral and political belief system to guide them in knowing what is important.

2.

In preparing to watch a TV news show, keep in mind that it is called a "show."

You may think that a TV news show is a public service and a public utility. But more than that, it is an enormously successful business enterprise. This does not mean that it is of no value. It means, first, that the "news" is only a commodity that is used to gather an audience which will be sold to advertisers; second, that the "news" is delivered as a form of entertainment (or at least, theater) because audiences find this palatable; and third, that the whole package is put together in the way that any theatrical producer would proceed, that is, by giving priority to show business values. In the case of most news shows the package includes attractive anchors, an exciting musical theme, comic relief (usually from the weather people, especially the men), stories placed to hold the audience, the creation of the illusion of intimacy, and so on. The point of this kind of show is that *no one is expected to take the news too seriously*. For one thing, tomorrow's news will have nothing to do with today's news. It is, in fact, best if the audience has completely

forgotten yesterday's news. TV shows work best by treat-
ing viewers as if they were amnesiacs.

3.
Never underestimate
the power of
commercials.

As we have emphasized, commercials are not fluff. They
are a serious form of popular literature, some would even
say a serious form of news. Upon being asked if TV news
is always bad news, Marshall McLuhan once remarked
that it is not; the commercials, he said, are the good
news. However we may label them, commercials tell as
much about our society as "straight" news does, probably more. We suspect that archaeologists studying the
artifacts of American culture two hundred years from
now will find our commercials the richest source of information about our fears, motivations, and exultations.
In any case, it is always of special interest for a viewer
to observe the contradictions between the messsages of
commercials and the messages of the news. In these contradictions, we may glimpse, pure if not serene, the social
and psychic dilemmas of our culture.

4.

Learn something about the economic and political interests of those who run TV stations.

This is not easy to do since it requires one to read industry publications, the *Wall Street Journal*, *Advertising Age*, and other related sources of information. But since we are going to suggest that you reduce by one-third your viewing of TV news (Recommendation 6), you might use the time saved to familiarize yourself with the backgrounds of those who are constructing the world for you. Keep in mind that other professionals—doctors, dentists, and lawyers, for example—commonly display their diplomas on their office walls to assure their clients that *someone* judged them to be competent. Granted, diplomas don't tell you much. (After all, half the doctors in America were, by definition, in the lower half of their graduating class.) But diplomas tell more than station "owners" and news directors and journalists tell. Wouldn't it be useful to know who these people are? Where they come from? What their angle is? And, especially, where they stand in relation to you? One doesn't have to be a Marxist to assume that people making a million dollars a year will see things differently from people struggling to make ends meet.

Our intention is not to encourage paranoia. We only wish to stress the point that the background of those who deliver the news to us is relevant to how we will judge what they say. At the very least you ought to give some thought to who owns the networks and some of the more important cable stations.

5.
Pay special attention to the language of newscasts.

Because film footage and other visual imagery are so engaging on TV news shows, viewers are apt to allow language to go unexamined. This is a mistake for several reasons, the most important of which is that a TV newscaster's language frames the pictures. As we have previously pointed out, a picture is by its nature a specific representation. However, what we are to make of the picture is often determined by the commentary made about it. Therefore, what is said requires careful attention. Since there are very few images that are self-explanatory, the viewer's attitude toward an image will be formed by words. There are limits, of course. A picture of a starving child cannot be converted into anything pleasant no matter how many words are used. But what the picture means must await commentary. Does the picture reflect the neglect of parents? The incompetence of politicians? The breakdown of an economic system? The callousness of the rich? These and other questions will be answered by the reporter's language. But this does not mean the explanation he or she gives is correct.

Another reason for attending to language is that reporters ask a lot of questions. A question is, after all, only a sentence. But it is a sentence that may reveal the biases and assumptions of the *questioner* as much as those of the person answering the question. Viewer alertness to the role that questions play in shaping answers was heightened during the Gulf War when audiences had an opportunity to listen to the questions reporters asked of military officials. Viewers could tell from the questions that many reporters knew very little about how the military operates during wartime. In fact, some of the questions were so inane and even nonsensical that "Saturday Night Live" made the press conferences the subject of a devastating satire. Of course, when there is no war, viewers are apt to let their guard down and pay little attention to the nature of the questions asked. Don't let this happen.

6.

Reduce by at least one-third the amount of TV news you watch.

In considering this suggestion, you might keep in mind the case of Ronny Zamora, whom we had occasion to mention in the chapter on television and the courts. Ronny's defense against the charge of murdering an old woman was that he was driven insane by watching too much violence on television. The jury rejected his claim but there is some value in your considering it. The Gerbner studies, also referred to before, clearly indicate that heavy viewing of TV news makes people think the world is much more dangerous than it actually is. The Kubey study indicates that watching television, including news shows, makes people somewhat more depressed than they would otherwise be. While habitual viewing of TV news may not make you insane, some believe it could turn you into a chronically depressed and constantly alarmed person.

Furthermore, if you are concerned that cutting down your viewing time will cause you to "miss" important news, keep this in mind: each day's TV news consists, for the most part, of fifteen or so *examples* of one or the other of the Seven Deadly Sins, with which you are already quite familiar. There may be a couple of stories exemplifying lust, usually four about murder, occasionally one about gluttony, another about envy, and so on. It cannot possibly do you any harm to excuse yourself each week from acquaintance with thirty or forty of these examples. Remember: TV news does not reflect normal, everyday life.

7.

Reduce by one-third the number of opinions you feel obligated to have.

One of the reasons many people are addicted to watching TV news is that they feel under pressure to have an opinion on almost everything. Middle-class people, at least those who are college educated, seem especially burdened by an unrealistic and slightly ridiculous obligation to have a ready-made opinion on any matter. For example, suppose you are attending a dinner party and someone asks you if you think the earth is undergoing permanent warming as a result of the depletion of the ozone layer. You are expected to say something like, "Absolutely. In fact, I heard a discussion of this on 'Nightline' last Thursday, and it looks as if we're in for devastating climatic changes." The fact is that you really don't know much about this matter, and "Nightline" only provides the most rudimentary and fragmented information about anything. Wouldn't it be liberating to be able to say when asked such a question, "I have no opinion on this since I know practically nothing about it"? Of course, we realize that if you gave such an answer five or six times during the course of a dinner party, you would probably not be asked back. But that would be a small price to pay for relieving yourself of the strain of storing thirty-two half-baked opinions to be retrieved at a moment's notice.

8.

Do whatever you can to get schools interested in teaching children how to watch a TV news show.

The best thing about "Channel One" is that it provides teachers with an opportunity to teach about news shows, about all the things we have written of in this book. It is surely not Whittle's intention that TV news be made into an object of study, and it is doubtful that teachers wish to do this. Nonetheless, it is not merely a good idea to do it, it is essential. The best way to prepare ourselves to know exactly what is happening (and why) when we watch a TV news show is to begin learning about it all when we are young. For reasons that defy understanding, our schools have not been enthusiastic about making inquiries into any aspect of television. Generally, teachers are willing to use television as an aid to learning (which is what Whittle wants them to do) but they have not been willing to study how television uses us. Anything you can do to reverse this disposition will be helpful. Of course, we would have no serious objections to your recommending our book.

INDEX